THE WALL

Alexander and Thomas Huber

A New Dimension in Climbing

Edited by Reinhold Messner
Foreword by Alan Hinkes

Translated by Tim Carruthers

THE WALL

David & Charles

"There is only one path to success: self-belief. The belief that I am capable of doing it!"

Alexander Huber

"Dreams are there to be dreamed
and turned into reality. If not today,
then maybe tomorrow."

Thomas Huber

CONTENTS

Foreword

Alex and Thomas Huber are both remarkable climbers, teaming up to make a formidable pair. I have had the pleasure of spending time with Alex. He exudes climbing; you can sense his devotion and enthusiasm for the 'Sport'. Like me, both Alex and Thomas are at home on the hills, whether in rock boots on a sun-drenched rock face, or in plastic boots and crampons on an ice face. As well as working as Mountain Guides in the Alps, they have climbed hard routes on vertical granite walls, limestone cliffs and summited an 8000m mountain in the Himalaya.

The pictures in this book give a dramatic insight into their special vertical, extreme world. The text is honest and bursting with realism. This is not just a book for fans of Alex and Thomas; their writing is accessible to less committed climbers.

The impressive list of ascents speaks for itself: extreme rock climbs on big walls, pushing the sport of rock climbing onto the enormous mountain faces.

There are autobiographical insights in places with flashbacks to the Hubers' beginnings, their early dreams, aspirations and influences, which are recorded and explained. Dedication to training is seen as a necessary means to an end.

Reinhold Messner salutes Alex and Thomas - what better accolade can there be? He appreciates their audacity and style as will any reader.

Alex and Thomas are true enthusiasts, real climbers with a big passion for the hills, mountains, crags and big rock faces. Other climbers will use this book as a benchmark to springboard the limits of big wall rock climbing still further.

Alan Hinkes

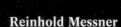

Reinhold Messner

In writing this book Alexander and Thomas Huber did not intend it to be their biography nor did they intend to deal exhaustively with the development of mountaineering. They are simply presenting their awareness of life as frontiersmen and they do it in a forthright and unembellished way. That is why I like them.

What is it that gives this book such explosive power? It is obvious: pictures which we have never seen before; texts which take our breath away; insights into a world which is, for all but a few of us, inaccessible.

The Huber brothers have not only pushed ahead with new dimensions of free climbing in the Eastern Alps, they have also opted to go for the difficult routes in the Karakorum and the Himalaya, even though many other professional mountaineers continue to increase their market value on the highly prestigious eight thousanders. On El Capitan's steepest wall in the Yosemite

Valley they have combined a route from parts of other routes which can be free climbed and suits their taste. In doing so they have rediscovered climbing and shown that, with highly trained muscles and strong reasoning, it is once again the spirit that defines the sport of mountaineering in the new millennium. Enthusiasm for the task and creativity in discovering and attacking big wall problems create a mentality which refuses to let doubt about one's actions surface at all.

Nevertheless the Hubers are self-critical; they speak openly about sibling rivalry, danger and leadership. Having grown up in a 'rope of four' with brothers (Günther, Siegfried and Hubert) myself, I know how difficult it is to speak openly of the emotions that drive us. I represented a type of mountaineering with a pinch of anarchy, for which I was condemned for thirty years by do-gooders and club stewards.

These days, when even self-professed outsiders are more concerned with their public image than the truth, if all weaknesses other than egocentric love of oneself were to remain hidden there would be no books such as this. In a time when people only pretend to be generous with information about themselves, when ghostwriters are engaged to make mountaineering books a market success, it takes courage to stand and bare one's soul before an audience which has an ever-decreasing insight into our world – a world which, to them, is becoming less and less accessible. As a mountaineer the decision to concentrate on one's climbs rather than on one's written works is comprehensible but books cobbled together by ghostwriters are just as damaging for mountaineering as invented trash journalism reports about the South Face of Lhotse, Cerro Torre and the Yeti.

The Huber brothers are as young as their achievements are outstanding. Sensible enough to dare to do 'the impossible' and blatantly bold, they have achieved glorious things, both individually and as a team. Dangerous and unique at the same time, their expeditions on Latok or the Ogre are revolutionary and their rock climbing on El Capitan accomplished. The Hubers are neither moralists, nor smug pedants for whom the history of mountaineering appears to be tainted; there is nothing half-hearted about them, and none of the self-righteous maliciousness which I dislike even more than empty boasting.

I am suspicious of innovators who, fearing that their innovations might act as a spur to others, preach mediocrity or cultivate their reputation as allies, without ever having to prove that they want anything other than intrigue. I hate them and I reject them. The Huber brothers' climbs awake in me neither envy nor resentment. They demand my wholehearted respect and they make me proud, proud of their actions which are beyond comparison.

Thomas and Alexander Huber do not do what the public expect from their heroes – no records, no Matterhorn, no Mount Everest – they do what they are best at and, although few people comprehend this, it still attracts a great deal of attention.

The innovators themselves are unaware of their own recipe for success. A modest childhood, a climbing father, early enthusiasm for the extreme, an understanding mother, systematic training, trips to the most difficult granite walls in the world are certainly prerequisites for the development of their curriculum vitae, and of their wholly unique style. They have rapidly become the forerunners of a young generation of frontiersmen seeking to solve the paradoxes of postmodern mountaineering by returning to the paradoxical venues frequented by their predecessors and, quite naturally, choosing the free route, the one that was too difficult for the oldtimers. Their instinct for the quality of the next step, and their decisiveness in making, it are what marks them out as members of the avant-garde. There is no pretence, they just do it and in so doing they shape the future. And that is exactly what this book does.

FREE SALATHÉ

ONE THOUSAND METRES OF VERTICAL GRANITE

A thousand metres of air beneath your feet: the first pitch of the Salathé Headwall, X-/5.13b, El Capitan, Yosemite/California, 1995 Alexander Huber

I first read Reinhard Karl's *Zeit zum Atmen* when I was fourteen years old. In fact, I devoured it at a single sitting. Not only because it was essential cult reading for climbers but because it really gripped me – more so than anything else I had ever read. As a young and ambitious climber I had a head full of dreams – the dreams that buzz around in your head, making you restless, creating desires and fantasies that are barely comprehensible. You marvel, you are seized by awe and wonderment. And you are jealous; you want to do these things too but you cannot – not yet.

I was looking for a role model, my idol, someone to show me what was possible. This someone was Reinhard Karl. It was not so much his ascent of Mount Everest that made him the idol of wild youth, but the diversity of his mountaineering achievements. This was world-wide mountaineering, not only confined to the Alps. His horizons extended much further, to the Himalayas, the Karakorum and to Patagonia, the mountain region with the worst weather and the most hellish storms in the world. And above all, his travels took him to sunny California, to the incomparable granite monolith of El Capitan in Yosemite, or 'the Valley' as we climbers affectionately refer to it – even a 14-year-old climber with a head full of nonsense.

For more than a hundred years, Yosemite's impressive cliffs have made it a Mecca for climbers. It was the big successes of the '60s – the first ascents of the big walls of El Capitan and Half Dome – that first cast the spotlight of the climbing world over the Valley. In those days, the man of the moment was without doubt Royal Robbins. He dominated events in the valley, and when other climbers' ideas on Yosemite climbing failed to match his own high standards he met the ensuing conflicts head on. Robbins was not only an immensely talented athlete. With his charisma and vision he made his mark, shaping the style of extreme climbing in the New Age – Big Wall climbing. In 1958 Warren Harding climbed the first ever Big Wall route with his first ascent of the Nose on El Capitan, but not without drawing harsh criticism from Robbins for the 125 expansion bolts he used. Robbins recognized even then the negative side to this development, commenting that ". . . any idiot could bolt his way up a Big Wall." With his first ascents in Yosemite, the no-compromise style of his repeats and his development of new Big Wall techniques, he defined the spirit of the age – and fought hard to preserve it. For more than twenty years, Royal Robbins was the undisputed leading light of the American climbing scene.

The seventies saw a new revolution in the sport of climbing. The Big Walls were no longer the standard by which all else was measured. Boulder problems like Midnight Lightning and routes like Separate Reality were the symbols; climbers like Ron Kauk and John Bachar the idols of the new generation; and 'free climbing' the message preached by the growing community of Yosemite climbers. They used artificial aids for protection only, not to make a sequence of moves possible. Climbers from every continent made their annual pilgrimage to Yosemite's Camp IV, where they indulged in 'the most important thing in the World' – climbing. Long before I ever visited Camp IV, I had already climbed many of the great Yosemite routes in my mind's eye, had risen above the horizontal world of mere mortals to pursue a single goal – the end of the climb. The more

obstacles I had to overcome in order to get there, the more intense the memories would be. With Reinhard Karl's books pointing the way, I dreamed of 50-metre traverses on poor pegs and tenuous skyhook placements; imagined myself, half dead with thirst, with bloody fingers and sweat-soaked, tattered clothing, pulling through the final few moves at the end of that trip to my personal separate reality, my alternative form of life.

be satisfied with anything less than a free ascent. Three years previously Lynn Hill had made a free ascent of the Nose; why then should I not attempt a free ascent of the Salathé?

Mid-April. Awestruck, I stand in the dust in the legendary Camp IV. English is only one language amongst many in this venerable old campsite. Climbers from all the nations of the World have come to Yosemite to climb – just like me, finally in the Valley to live out my dreams. And I am not disappointed. Even if my search for the heroes of days past is in vain, I find traces of the magic of the old days everywhere. On every route I climb I can scent something of the famous past of Yosemite climbing.

High up on El Cap, on the Sous Le Toit ledge – a tiny perch 40 metres below the big roof at the beginning of the famous Headwall of the Salathé – Gottfried Wallner and I have set up a bivouac occupying less than one square metre. There is not enough room here for even one of us to lie down. Nevertheless, we promise ourselves a pleasant bivi, sitting next to one another in our sleeping bags. The night is warm and cloudless. Cloudless! I am just twisting myself around into the best position for sleeping when suddenly, in the truest sense of the words 'out of the blue', it starts to pour with rain. Even before Gottfried can free himself from his sleeping bag, the weather ghost has gone again and we are soaking wet. We sit in silence next to each other, gazing up in bewilderment into the darkness. I am just searching around in the rucksack for the torch when a second brief shower dumps on us. Damn it! In the beam of the torch we can make out a streak of melt water which ends at a huge roof to the right of the Salathé Headwall, 100 metres

At first, they remained just dreams. The inexhaustible challenges of the Alps were too close at hand, while the Yosemite Valley in California remained just too distant. Then, in 1995, a plan was hatched for an expedition to the granite towers of the Latok group in the Karakorum. The obvious thing to do was to learn how to climb on granite – systematically. Although I had done first ascents of some of the hardest limestone routes in the world, climbing granite cracks had about as

◆ **I NOW REALIZED THAT MY DREAM WAS POSSIBLE –
TO FREE CLIMB ONE OF THE TRULY GREAT ROUTES IN THE WORLD**

much in common with the pockets and tiny crimps of limestone as the gymnastic disciplines of the pommel horse and the high bar have with each other. A solid regime of preparation was called for; a strict training programme, in other words.

And so it was that the opportunity for a Big Wall trip to Yosemite now presented itself. However, I was no longer the slightest bit interested in climbing any old route on El Capitan in any old style. In this respect, I now had very concrete ideas. I had become too much of a free climber to

above and 50 metres to the right of our little perch. During the day this waterfall had remained hidden from view; the strong valley wind in Yosemite had sent the cold wet deluge in the opposite direction. But as the the sun set, the wind direction changed and the mountain wind was now responsible for the irregular showers and increasingly frequent soakings we were getting.

I had had quite enough water already. Since my arrival in Yosemite Valley the weather had been characterized by rain, snow and floods. 'Below normal temperatures and above normal chance of rain', the weather report in the newspapers had been saying for the last six weeks, and, for a change, it was absolutely spot on. Accordingly, El Capitan looked more like a vertical waterfall chute than a brilliant place to climb.

At the Ear, an ear-shaped flake detached from the main mass of the cliff, I had already had my first taste today of climbing through the water; during the late afternoon I got a second opportunity, this time on the waterfall pitch below the Block, a bivi

Two monolithic granite walls converge at 90 degrees to each other – layback techniques on the perfect Headwall Dihedral, 5.12d

ledge 700 metres above the valley floor. Since the Block did not seem to offer enough protection from the various waterfalls, we thought we would be better and more safely accommodated on the tiny Sous Le Toit ledge below the roof. But there could be no thought of sleep, and in the morning everything was soaked through – sleeping bags, clothing, climbing gear, boots. . . . At first light, we forced our tortured, chilled and stiff bodies up

onto the exposed Headwall, the last pitches of the Salathé. Towards midday, we topped out on the summit plateau, totally drained. Warm sunlight at last, and finally an end to the toil.

Nevertheless, the trip had been a valuable experience. I now realized that my dream was possible – to free climb one of the truly great routes in the World.

For years, Thomas and I had been discussing a trip to California to free climb one of the big El Cap routes. Back in 1988 Todd Skinner and Paul Piana had caused a huge uproar when they claimed the first free ascent of the Salathé. Over a period of several weeks they allegedly climbed all of the pitches free, but the 'scene' expressed doubts as to their claim. Skinner and Piana rated the long, slim dihedral leading to El Cap Spire, a free-standing tower at two-thirds height on the face, at 5.13a on the American grading system.

But the pitch turned out to be a real stopper. Plenty of climbers, in particular prominent players like Stefan Glowacz, failed on it. Obviously the dihedral was far more difficult than the grade suggested by Skinner would suggest. This gross

◆ THE HEADWALL: A WALL WITHIN A WALL

factual error of judgement at the upper limit of the climber's art at the time gave the grounds for the doubts expressed about a completely free ascent of the Salathé in 1988.

From El Cap Meadows, the huge field at the foot of the wall, I had already spotted a wide crack running up some six metres to the left of the original dihedral. A thin undercling dropping away down and left along a flake would allow a spacy traverse to be made – it would go at about grade IX – out of the original line to join a 50-metre long, horribly strenuous body-width crack system. And thus draw the sting out of the first crux.

Then there was the Headwall. Cold and wet after our grandiose night bivouacking in a waterfall, I had been unable to climb even a single metre of it free but even so I could still see that my project was possible. There was no doubt about it; the Headwall – and thus the Salathé – would go free. I could do it.

Sunny California! I rained, it snowed, and I waited a whole week down in the Yosemite Valley before the weather gods finally seemed to see things my way. The weather report predicted rather changeable weather for the coming days but the general forecast was good. I was ready. Loaded up with 200 metres of fixed rope, bivouac equipment and food for five days – a total of more than 30 kilos on my back – I climbed alone up the East Ledges to the summit of El Capitan. I had hardly reached the bivouac site under a little rock roof on the summit plateau when I was caught in the downpour – how could it have been any different? Unfortunately, I was badly equipped for such an eventuality; I had neither a tent nor waterproof clothing with me. Although the roof offered me some measure of protection from the rain, my clothes were soon completely soaked through. In the middle of the night the wind blew up and a short while later snowflakes were whipping around my ears; a cold front with massive snowfalls was on its way towards me. If I wished to avoid the threat of hypothermia I had to think of something fast. So off I went through the driving snow in search of a drier spot to bivi. After a short time, as luck would have it, I discovered a small cave; an ideal place, since I would certainly not find anywhere more sheltered on the bare high plateau of the El Cap summit. First of all, though, I had to use a stick to remove the already rotting carcass of a large bird from my cave. For two days I toughed it out in my sparse 'hotel room', constantly massaging the cold from my limbs, brooding and plagued by doubts, before the fine weather that had been forecast finally provided me with some relief.

I spent the following days doing nothing else than hanging on jumars studying the moves on the Headwall. According to Todd Skinner's reports it went free in three pitches, two of 5.13a and one of 5.13b. However, the Skinner stance between the first two pitches was a hanging belay on new bolts, and this was something I wished to avoid at all costs, since it contravened our personal climbing ethics, which stipulated the use of 'no-hands rests' only for belays to avoid making the climb easier by splitting pitches into shorter sections. So I ran the first two Headwall pitches together. It was also my intention to free climb the Salathé in one push, in as few days as possible, redpointing all the pitches;

The countdown begins – on the last stance before the start of the Headwall

in other words, leading each pitch clean and with no falls and placing all the necessary protection on the crack sections on the lead.

The Headwall. A wall within a wall, the crux of the Salathé. A V-shaped crack forms the start. Free climbing on the tiniest crimps up rounded edges. The start of the main crack is gained by a jump, 900 metres above El Cap Meadows, but by then you have long since got used to the dizzying view down, the abyss sucking at your heels. The crack splits the Headwall, 70 metres without rest or respite. Up to the first no-hands rest, which arrives after 55 metres and signals the end of the first pitch of free climbing, the climbing difficulties are pretty much dominated by flared handjams. The second, considerably shorter, pitch kicks off with an exquisite finger crack, fading after a second no-hands rest to an incipient crack which only succumbs to face climbing techniques. Hard work indeed.

17

FREE CLIMBING TERMINOLOGY

What is Free Climbing?

In the 'Sport for All' age free climbing is often confused with climbing without a rope. Free climbing simply means the exclusive use of the natural rock features in order to make progress, as distinct from artificial climbing, where artificial (technical) aids are used to make progress; here, pitons and artificial chockstones are placed in cracks and etriers (ladders) clipped to them as the climber slowly makes his way up the route, metre by metre.

In climbing jargon, climbing alone is known as 'soloing', regardless of whether the climber is using a self-belay system or not. Climbing alone without a rope, often widely misunderstood to be free climbing, is more correctly referred to as 'free soloing'.

Redpoint:

A no-falls ascent of a route on the lead (belayed from below), where the climber only makes use of the natural rock features for holds.

Yo-Yoing:

An ascent of a route on the lead, where the climber only makes use of the natural rock features for holds. However, in contrast to redpointing, the rope may be left clipped into a high piece of protection reached fall-free from a previous attempt and used as protection for the ascent.

On sight:

A redpoint ascent of an 'unknown' route, climbed on the first attempt. The route may only be inspected from the ground; in order to claim an on-sight ascent, other climbers may not be observed on the route and no information about the route may be sought from others.

Flash:

A redpoint ascent of an 'unknown' route, climbed on the first attempt. However, in contrast to the on-sight ascent, the climber may have prior information ('beta') about the route; for example, he may have observed others climbing it or asked other climbers about it.

Free Solo:

A rope-free solo ascent of a route, whereby the climber places no protection and makes exclusive use of the natural rock features in order to make progress.

Toprope:

An ascent of a route with the protection of the climbing rope anchored from above. In free climbing parlance, however, a route is only considered to have been 'done' if it has been led free.

No-hand-rest:

A point on a route where the climber can rest without the use of the arms.

On the first pitch of the Headwall – the calm before the storm; nerves stretched to breaking point

And once again, flakes of snow are flying around my ears, so I quit El Capitan with all due speed, not wanting to have yet another unpleasant bivouac forced upon me.

Waiting for the fine weather, a whole week long. Finally I went back up, but this time with a tent. Like a gymnast working on his routine, I worked the moves once again until, two days later, Yosemite veteran Mark Chapman paid me a visit and offered to belay me as I led these crux pitches. We abseiled down the last five pitches to the start of the Headwall. I was nervous, damned nervous. Even so, as I began the first pitch I started to concentrate. Everything around me was soon forgotten, my thoughts focussed only on the next move, my field of vision narrowed down so that I saw only the next jam, the next hold. Finally, three metres from the belay, I placed my last nut. Strength ebbing fast, I tugged at the rope. Nothing, no movement; the tremendous rope drag prevented me clipping the rope into the carabiner, and the last piece of protection was ten metres below me. And the next few metres were the hardest. . . .

There was only one thing for it: escape had to be upwards, with a 20-metre fall staring me in the face. At first you think everything is just conspiring against you and then later you have no real idea how you managed it. Maybe it was just stubbornness on my part. "Hey you guy, that runout was fuckin' crazy, man!" Mark congratulated me, shaking his head. Two hours later we were celebrating with Budweiser and potato crisps on the top for the first redpoint ascent of possibly the best pitch in the world.

I was now ready for the final complete redpoint. I was soon standing at the foot of El Cap again,

this time with Heinz Zak. Bad weather put an end to the first attempt; once more St. Peter was merciless and a cloudburst washed us back down to terra firma. So we waited in the Valley until the meteorologists announced the end of the 'rainy season'.

Now, for the n-th time, I climbed the first, easy-angled, third of the Salathé. Reaching the legendary Hollow Flake, a 30-metre chimney with no means of protection, we caught up with a slower party, who had been grappling with the pitch for some considerable time. The overtaking manoeuvres were complicated by a lack of understanding. "It's my only week of vacation and all I wanna have is fun!" And 'fun' quite obviously did not include being overtaken by another team. Thus the overtaking manoeuvres ended in chaos and cost both parties time and nervous energy.

The off-width crack below El Cap Spire also cost us precious time and nerves. It was the nastiest kind of crack – just too narrow to disappear inside

A continuous 70-metre crack splits the granite here at the first pitch of the Salathé Headwall, 5.13b

and much too wide to get an efficient jam with any part of your body between the parallel walls. And as for protection – forget it! For a crack of this width all conventional protection devices are too small. Forty metres of climbing with illusory protection and the rope serves merely as moral support. The fall potential gets more spectacular the higher you go – almost 100 metres at the end of the pitch – not something I would necessarily recommend.

The moves are abnormal; abnormally strenuous, abnormally irritating and abnormally time-consuming. It's a horror-show; inch by inch you scrape your way upwards, heading towards release and redemption. It's a real battle, and it is just this confrontation with oft-quoted adventure that we are searching for in this vertical world.

◆ I SCREAM MY JOY TO THE WORLD

At 6:00 PM I arrive at El Cap Spire, pumped ragged and totally spent, but happy that this pitch is finally behind me. Five pitches above us is the Block, the next bivouac and today's objective. At the last big hurdle, the 5.12d pitch shortly below the Block, it happens. For two minutes I hang there on small crimps; I can no longer remember the correct solution to the sequence, a cross-through move. As I grow more nervous the right sequence of moves becomes blurred in my mind; I fight on desperately, muscles burning. At some point I am no longer capable of doing anything more; I fall off backwards, the rope dragging at my climbing harness. I can't believe it! I try the moves three more times, until I finally find the solution. Jumping off one more time, I make another attempt at climbing the whole pitch without falls. No rest for the wicked! Darkness is falling fast, there really isn't enough time, my arms are tired – time to give it a go. . . .

I manage the cross-through move and carry on, only the overhanging dihedral to do now. My arms have nothing more to give and my fingers keep cramping up. The only thing that is still half working is my footwork; it gets me up the final few metres. It is already dark as Heinz and I sort ourselves out for our bivouac on the Block. Slowly, the feeling dawns on me that I have made some big, decisive steps.

The next day comes. There are only ten pitches above us, so we have lots of time. I have a really long lie-in and it is midday by the time I set off, somewhat stiffly, on the first pitch to the Sous Le Toit ledge. Although not too hard it nevertheless demands a great deal from me. It takes a while before I feel, with relief, the fresh blood rinsing the trash of the previous day from my lower arms.

At the start of the Headwall I am tremendously nervous and after only a few metres I take a fall trying to do the dyno into the main crack. Annoyed with myself, I have to force myself to calm down, otherwise I will never manage it. Slowly, I become calmer, the tension evaporates and I start up the pitch again. After my experience on the trial run with Mark Chapman, the plan this time is to dispense with the last but one piece of protection in order to save strength to place and clip the last piece. I'm not into running it out like 'fuckin' crazy' on this, the crux of the route. As I am placing this last bit of gear my hand slips in the crack – I do not need to look down to know there's a 20-metre whipper waiting for me, I can feel it like ice on the back of my neck. I press my fingers even harder into the crack, using strength I did not know I had. Motivation, maybe? Or adrenaline? Everything is reduced down to this one crack, this one finger jam. El Cap for me is now only a matter of these few moves; the crack has become a microcosm in the unending, featureless wilderness of its granite walls.

With every ounce of strength I have I bore the thin edge of my fingertips into the narrow crack and twist my fingers through a full 90 degrees, ignoring the pain. This is pure masochism. There are four moves like this, all on the fingertips. You go for it, you don't notice or feel anything any more, you just want to get out of there. And you make it . . .

In spite of the pain in my fingers, I scream my joy to the world, drunk on adrenaline.

Topping out on the Salathé, on the summit plateau of El Capitan, I stare down at the valley below and draw deeply on the success of having found a solution to one of the greatest challenges modern free climbing has to offer. Eyes wide open, I gaze down into the Valley, yet I see nothing. The inner film starts playing, a film about a dance up a thousand metres of granite.

The next move – the micrcosm of a climber adrift on an endless sea of El Cap granite. This is the second pitch of the Salathé Headwall, 5.13b

FREE SALATHÉ
TAKE TWO

Thomas Huber

During the winter of 1994-95 the Free Salathé project became more tangible for Alexander and I; it started to take on a more concrete character. We were both training hard for our common objective; it took over completely, forcing us to do specialized power-endurance training sessions. One thousand metres of vertical rock of the quality of the Salathé meant that this was a clear necessity. Then, suddenly, my passion for snowboarding ruined everything. I was going too fast, took a fall and my knee was a complete write-off: a torn cruciate ligament, both meniscus crushed, the capsules in the popliteal space torn to shreds . . .

Alexander flew off to California on his own to realize our El Cap plan, the plan we had once shared. Meanwhile, I lay in my hospital bed in the University Hospital of Innsbruck – 3rd floor, Surgical Ward, 3rd room on the left – with a marvellous view of the crags of the Martinswand opposite. My thoughts circled like the hang-gliders soaring on the evening thermals before that yellow-grey wall; the Martinswand became El Capitan, I lost myself in my fantasies and dreamed of sunny California, felt the warmth of the El Cap rock and saw my brother climbing the knife-sharp cracks of the Salathé.

I had to drift off into an irrational world of my own, otherwise I would not have been able to cope with the situation in which I found myself. The reality was that I was shackled to a hospital bed, my leg bandaged up and strapped to a splint, while two drainage tubes sucked the secretions from my freshly-operated knee. I was condemned to a period of inactivity; I could only dream of the Salathé. I cursed myself for an idiot; if only I had gone into that steep section more slowly; damned snowboard; if only I had . . .

But it was all pointless, it had been my own lack of caution that had caused the Salathé Dream to burst like a soap bubble. In my mind's eye, I toyed with thoughts of the Martinswand opposite and knew that Alexander would be successful – without me. He would write a new chapter in El Capitan history – without me. 'Alexander Huber: Free Salathé' it would read, while I lay here in hospital, within the sterile confines of these four white walls.

I awaited the outcome with feverish anticipation yet was at the same time jealous of him. If I wished success on anyone then I wished it on Alexander. I did not begrudge him this yet the knowledge that I would not be there to share in it gnawed away at me at the same time. I vowed to attempt it, too, as soon as this knee started functioning again, as soon as I was able to climb again, if I could regain my old form, and if . . . if . . . I would emulate Alexander – I had to, that was the only comfort I had, together with the certainty that Alexander would manage it. When I finally heard that he had indeed redpointed that superb route I looked out from my sick bed at my wall and cried. I was happy for him and at odds with myself – what would I not have given to stand up on top of El Cap with him! Alexander visited me during my rehabilitation in Innsbruck. He told me about the Salathé, I told him about the state of my health and the progress I was making. I could already walk on crutches and in a couple of months maybe I would be allowed to climb again. That was the light at the end of the tunnel for me, the strip of silver light on the far horizon, as far away as the Salathé on El Capitan.

One year later I was in the Yosemite Valley. My premiere was on the granite colossus of El Capitan. This first encounter was going to be something special – at least that is what I had planned. So there I was, 800 metres above the valley floor, grappling with the Headwall of the Salathé. I got a lot of helpful beta from my brother about the Free Salathé project but it still took more than a month before I felt fit enough to climb that 1000-metre Big Wall free in one push. For his redpoint ascent, Alexander had opted for a time-scale of three days and a 50-metre variant up a monster off-width crack below El Cap Spire, in order to avoid the most difficult pitch, the Double Crack. To be honest, my presumptuous objective was a one-day redpoint ascent incorporating the original dihedral pitch, the Double Crack. It was an ambitious goal, and one on which, realistically speaking, I was bound to lose. After many failed attempts I was finally able to wring out a pretty poor redpoint with the gear in place and clipped – my last chance, shortly before my return flight to Germany. Two of the pitches I was only able to climb after several falls, starting again each time from no-hands rests in the middle of the pitch, and the single-day free ascent finally ended up taking one and a half days.

 MY SENSE OF REALITY HAD BEEN CLOUDED BY AMBITION

Alexander's was clearly the better ascent. He had managed an undisputed redpoint of the Salathé in a considerably shorter time and was more than happy with his performance. I, on the other hand, had bet everything on one card. Instead of doing the same thing that had brought Alexander his success, a redpoint ascent spread over three days with three bivis on the face and avoiding the Double Crack, my deeds had been driven by my emotions. I wanted too much, I wanted it all; I especially wanted to compensate for my privations of the last year with a spectacular one-day redpoint ascent of the original line of the Salathé. And I paid for it. I was not happy with my ascent. I had presumably dreamed the dream for too long; day by day it had grown more and more presumptuous until it reached the point at which it was no longer a realisable aim for me, at least not at the time. But my sense of reality had been clouded by ambition and I did not realize that I had set my target a touch too high.

Dreams are there to be dreamed and turned into reality. If not today, then maybe tomorrow.

A family affair – one year on, same mountain, same route.
Thomas on the second pitch of the Headwall, 5.13b

PATHS INTO UNCERTAINTY
RAUNACHTS

**New territory: on the third pitch of
Raunachtstanz on the Wagendrischlhorn,
Berchtesgaden/Germany, 1984
Thomas Huber**

Our joint climbing career begins early. Even as little kids we are out and about in the mountains with the family and our father soon takes us lads out rock climbing and mountaineering with him, laying in us the foundation stones of the all-round alpinist. More and more, however, our passions are directed towards the cliffs and soon both of us use every opportunity offered to go climbing.

Alexander and I soon become a well-honed team. Neither of us has yet reached the age of maturity and so our biggest problem is actually getting to the mountains at all. Although our home town, Palling, lies in the Chiemgau and on fine days, from the Pallinger Berg, a nearby wooded hill, we can even see the mountain peaks from the Dachstein to the Zugspitze so clearly we could almost reach out and touch them, without a driving licence and our own car they remain unreachable for us. Unreachable, too, because Palling was obviously forgotten by those responsible for planning local public transport facilities in Upper Bavaria. There is no bus, and no train – only the inn 'Zum Bahnhof' reminds us of better times for immobile young climbers. And to

TANZ

set off on our pushbikes for the hills, like the heroes of the 'thirties, is, despite all the love we have for our sport and for nature, not really our thing. So we are dependent upon getting lifts, lifts which do not always materialize. Then we suffer and turn to the only other available climbing, the well-formed apple tree in the garden.

Necessity being the mother of invention, in our mind's eye the tree mutates into an extreme Alpine face and the whole range of technical tricks is employed: overhangs are free climbed, and we set

summit. According to the first ascent team the difficulties lie in the upper grade V region; in other words, moderately hard climbing but we know from the tales of other climbers that Heinz Mariacher grades his routes very harshly. The information in the climbing guidebook says it all really: 'Rather loose in parts, with long and bold sections of free climbing. A few nuts required; poor pegs'. Straight from the mouth of the current climbing élite. The Via Niagra promises to be just what we are looking for.

◆ ALEXANDER AND I, ON THE OTHER HAND, ARE AFTER ADVENTURE

up hanging belays in slings and free abseils. The apple tree offers a total of eight routes, all named after the great classic extremes of the Alps: The Comici Route on the Cima Grande, South Face of the Torre Triest, Carlesso . . . We act out everything we have read in Alpine literature, even the tragic end that befell Toni Kurz on the Eigerwand is faithfully reconstructed so that in an emergency we would at least know the ropework in the event that a similar situation were to happen to us. The only thing missing is a bivi in slings in the tree, but that really would be taking things a bit too far – not for us, but for our mother.

When we do then get into the mountains we are often out and about with our father and his climbing partner Rainer. While they go off to climb some pleasant classic or other we tend to prefer sterner fare, routes on which we find the challenge of being able to test our boundaries, adventures laced with a generous portion of fear. Our pleasure is retrospective, as we recall our hair-raising experiences.

The summer holidays of 1984 see us escaping from the Berchtesgaden Alps to climb in the Dolomites. Father and Rainer are doing the Fedele Route on the Pordoispitze, a grade IV route taking in some impressive scenery. Alexander and I, on the other hand, are after adventure. To the left of the Fedele is a black wall, often wet. This is the line of the Via Niagara, first climbed in 1978 by Heinz Mariacher and Luisa Jovane. We have heard a lot of wild stuff about this route, and very little that is good, and that is exactly why it is such a challenge for us. According to the description, it goes up the right-hand edge of a waterfall, a whole 400 metres of overhanging rock with virtually no protection pegs. Even after the big rubble terrace there are still 200 metres of extremely loose rock to the

We climb into uncertain territory. Almost everything looks the same; above us, just black, overhanging rock with no signs of anyone having climbed here and no visible pegs to show us the way. The most important point of reference for us is the difficulty of the climbing which, according to the topo, nowhere exceeds the upper grade V level. We have to trust our feelings. The estimated standard of difficulty is generally the only aid to orientation on this face. When the forearms get pumped and the whole body starts shaking it is obvious that the climbing is harder than grade V and we are off-route. If the lower arms are supple and well supplied with blood, the moves accomplished efficiently and smoothly, then the actual difficulties are in agreement with the information on the topo and we even find the odd hidden piton on the Via Niagara.

Alexander leads the first crux pitch. According to the topo this leads to a stance in a little niche after a leftwards traverse. 30 metres vertically above me, Alexander starts out across the traverse and disappears around an arête. Verbal communication is interrupted, the rope runs through the belay crab a centimetre at a time. Time passes, nothing happens. Now and then there is a tug on the rope, more of a nervous twitch really, and I assume from this that Alexander is having to fight for every centimetre. It must be hard. I hold the rope tight in my hand, constantly aware that the very next second it might be pulled as taught as a guitar string. After half an eternity the rope goes slack. It seems that Alexander has given up. He looks back around the corner and curses. He has found the niche, guarded by an overhang, but he was unable to pull over this into it. He is just 20 centimetres short of the crucial hand hold, he reckons.

He rages at the injustice of it all, stopped dead in his tracks simply because of his lack of reach.

The Dolomites – breathtaking steepness and good holds, a
superbly rich source of great climbs.
Alexander on the Comici on the North Face of the Cima Grande

Alexander is in a stinking mood, the usual state of affairs for him when confronted by a seemingly insurmountable obstacle on the rock. But it is also a good sign, because anger lends him wings allowing him to find the enormous psychological strength that gets him through problems like this. His annoyance at being dealt an unfair size disadvantage (Alexander, at 15, is 1 metre 50 tall) gradually gives way to a rational assessment of the situation and he looks for the weak point which, according to his theory, all seemingly impossible sequences have. Imagination, a keen mind and a keener eye are all it takes to find it. This time is no different; he climbs back up three metres higher than before and starts the traverse again from that point. Again he disappears from view, again the anxious waiting, interminable minutes long until, after a tortured quarter of an hour, the signal comes that he is on belay.

I second the pitch. Respect is due. At the stance, a brief handshake for a notable performance, then we are off again, climbing quickly now to avoid wasting any more time. Pitch after pitch, we climb higher, always on the lookout for the ideal line. Towards evening, after eight hours of climbing, we meet up with Father and Rainer on the top. They tell us about the very pleasant experience they had on the Fedele and we report on our adventure on the Via Niagara. Two parties, two fundamentally very different climbs, but all four of us have one thing in common: a wonderful, exciting and thoroughly pleasurable day in the mountains has enriched our memories.

The remaining days of our holiday follow a similar pattern: hike up to the start of the route, unpack the sack, have a bite to eat. A quick look up at the

28

The Berchtesgaden Alps are the
stuff of which dreams are made

route – "It's a steep one!" – a little anxious at the start. Harness on, tie into the rope with a figure-of-eight knot, squeeze into too-tight rock boots, sort out the gear and rack it on the harness, helmet on and off we go . . . rock, rock, undercling rock, flat hold, rock, awkward bit, arms getting pumped, fear – "Watch me here, Alexander! – hang the little crimp, done it!" – "Thomas, you've only got two

formations like cracks, buttresses and grooves, is a coveted prize and we have even heard of climbers coming to blows over it. Alexander and I have no wish to provoke a war – what the others do not know will not make them jealous.

Pregnant with our ideas, we carry them silently around with us, waiting only for the time when we are strong enough to put an end to millions of

◆ THIS SOUTH FACE IS THE OBJECT OF OUR AMBITIOUS PLANS

metres of rope!" – "On belay, Alexander! Come on!" – "Climbing!" – "Good effort, Thomas!" – and onwards . . . rock . . . an hour, rock . . . two hours, rock . . . three hours, rock . . . and on and on . . . the last pitch, the top. Handshakes, descent, abseil, happiness . . . a last look back and a new plan for the next day. . . .

We had never before done so much climbing. Apart from a few days' rain we spend the whole summer holidays climbing and we really ought to be well satisfied with our summer haul of routes. But we are too good now – and also too self-confident – to ignore the fact that there was something missing from the heady brew. We are not really concerned about climbing a specific, even harder, route. The challenge no longer lies in repeating a further dozen demanding climbs or in doing something of extreme difficulty in another climbing area. What we are after is a route which as yet has no description and no information about the line it takes, the level of difficulty or the character. A route that, to begin with, exists only in our dreams. A voyage of discovery into a vertical rock landscape. 'Unexplored new territory' – a bland term but for us it embodies the great hidden secret of the sport of mountaineering.

The myth of rock as yet untouched gradually changes into a tangible experience. The first step in this process, a new dimension for us, is the search for a suitable objective. There is plenty of vertical no-man's land available but the great art lies in recognizing the worthwhile lines on these rock bastions. It is the creative, searching look that etches a hitherto invisible line into the cliff. Hardly a day passes in the mountains when we do not project our craziest ideas onto the rock walls before us. We protect and cherish these new discoveries like precious treasure and keep them totally secret. Attractive new ground, a route up an as yet unclimbed wall or following prominent rock

Raunachtstanz: Mother Nature provides the line, we provide the name

years of untouched rock, to be the first to feel it. To begin with, the very idea seems presumptuous, insolent even – who are we to disturb the natural order of things? We justify our project in the unique fashion common to every new route attempt: to enter into an adventure, the outcome of which can barely be calculated.

At the end of the holidays, before school again limits our freedom, we intend to use our good climbing form and our newly strengthened sense of self-confidence to take the next big step in our young, yet intensive, lives as climbers. We want to feel that new territory between the fingers, climb along the path to total uncertainty. Up to now such thoughts have only been the subject of my day-dreams – the last piece of protection several metres below, above me full-on grade VII climbing, my absolute limit, rock boots sliding on two friction holds, fingers clawing at at tiny edge, no holds above me and not even the slightest possibility of placing more gear . . . a frightening image, but that is why it exerts such a fascination. Nothing can stop us now; we are about to take that step into new territory.

The focus of our desires is the South Face of the Wagendrischlhorns on the Reiteralm. Although a mere 250 metres high, and not even particularly steep, the rock is compact and of the best quality. Above all, however, the light-coloured slabs are scored by beautiful erosion flutings. This South Face is the object of our ambitious plans. Just a few weeks ago one of 'our' lines there was claimed – we do not intend to let anyone snatch another one from us!

The first crux is our lack of mobility. Here, Alexander's powers of persuasion are called for. He attempts to explain to our mother that one last pleasant little climb at the end of the holidays would be a great motivator for our return to school and that nothing would improve our scholastic performance more than a relaxing day out in the

FREE CLIMBING GRADING
SYSTEM

The rating system used to describe the degree of difficulty of free climbs is, like the Richter Scale for earthquakes, an open-ended system. The harder the route, the higher the difficulty rating. In Germany, the scale uses Roman numerals and currently ranges from I to XI. Within each individual grade, the addition of a + or - allows for further fine-tuning. Thus, a VII+ is more difficult than a VII and a VII harder than a VII-.

Grading the difficulty of a free climb is basically a subjective matter. When a route is first climbed the first ascentionist will give it a suggested rating. This suggestion is based on the personal feeling of the first ascentionist about the difficulty of the route, compared to other established route on the scale. If the first ascentionist requires roughly the same amount of time to complete his redpoint as he does for a grade VIII route he will suggest this as the grade for his new route. If, however, he needs double the time he will grade his route slightly harder, say VIII+.

Over time, repeats of the route will give rise to several grade suggestions and these may differ considerably from the rating suggested by the first person to climb it. The final grade will be the result of concensus opinion and generally a high degree of objectivity can be attributed to this rating. There are several systems currently in use internationally and these can be directly compared in tabular form. The most important are the French system, the UIAA system used in Germany and the American system (see page 128).

hills. After a bit of to-ing and fro-ing he actually manages to persuade her. She will chauffeur us to Reit the next day, the starting point for our project, a project with the thinly-veiled working title 'a nice little grade V climb'.

That evening, Alexander and I sit in the attic and study a slide of 'our' rock face projected onto the wall. With painstaking attention to detail, we attempt to identify the points of weakness in the big sweep of slabs. Finally we take a sheet of paper and make a sketch of the best possible, though still approximate, line.

That night, there can be no thought of sleep, we are far too excited. Questions follow questions, doubts surface. Are we really good enough? Again this image of mine intrudes – my boots sliding, not a hold in sight . . . Then Alexander's axiom kicks

WE ARE ABOUT TO TAKE A STEP INTO NEW TERRITORY

in again – there is always a weakness to be exploited. What do those slabs hold in store for us? And if we really do manage it? I toss and turn in my bed. It all feels very different to the usual thoughts the day before a hard route; the feeling of uncertainty is overpowering. How I would love to just give in to bland fatalism, just 'have a look and see what happens' – and again my foot slides off the friction smear.

It is still dark as Mother drives us to Reit. We have to promise her once again to be careful and only to do an easy route. Feigning innocence and keeping a straight face we give her our word. Perhaps our project will even turn out to be easier than we assumed and our promise will reflect the truth?

An hour after sunrise Alexander and I are standing at the bottom of the route, the nervousness of the night long since forgotten. Now comes the crunch. As we look up at the slabs our fictitious line begins to take shape, yes, it should go, and this calms the nerves even if Alexander's only comment is "Steep!".

He climbs the relatively easy first pillar. Beyond this, the wall becomes featureless and compact. Here he hands over the lead to me, bowing to my greater experience. I rack the gear, clip it to my harness, prepare myself and check everything one last time: harness, knot, my thoughts . . . The adventure begins. I take a deep breath and set off into the unknown.

Eight metres above the belay I hammer a standard piton into the solid rock and traverse to the left on good holds across the otherwise featureless wall. Although the difficulties nowhere exceed grade VI my movements are rather more restrained than usual, my climbing more focused and precise than is normally the case. I cannot allow myself to get sloppy or to make a mistake here. High up and left a smooth section of slab interrupts the flow of my climbing. Only now do I realize that a fall could have unhealthy consequences and that so far I have been climbing in blinkers. It is hard to hold onto the 'what is below does not matter to me when it is up there I want to be' idea for very long so I place another peg. Hypersensitized as I am now, I do not trust it on its own and back it up with a nut. I want 100% reliable protection here, otherwise the next bit would be potentially fatal.

I creep leftwards across the holdless slab and after three shaky metres at the limit of sole adhesion I latch the next good hold at the start of a lovely, deep erosion fluting. The next two pitches are exciting, but not as challenging as the slab below. Wide, water-worn channels and heavily featured slabs give beautiful climbing and land us at a broad terrace. So far, everything has gone well, the path to uncertainty in every way indentical to the line we had envisaged.

Now, however, it looks as if things are getting serious, more serious even than down there on the second pitch. Two parallel, shallow water-worn flutings run for 30 metres up a steep, compact wall to a small ledge. This will be the crux, not only as regards pure difficulty but also from the point of view of danger. This double fluting seems to be just about unprotectable, it is just too shallow to take any gear. My heart sinks. Time to take a break on the ledge. Actually it is a really nice place, with green padding to sit on, sun, blue skies and the total solitude of a wild mountain landscape.

I am incapable of enjoying it, however. I have got a queasy feeling in my stomach. At the moment I am concerned with one thing only, the next 30 metres above us. Alexander munches a muesli bar, looks across to Leoganger Alps and informs me, in all seriousness, that he has seen another possible new line over there on the Birnhorn. Were I not completely absorbed with the uncertainty of the climbing above I would surely grab him by the throat! How on earth can he prattle on about another new route when we have not even done the first one yet, when we are right slap-bang in the middle of it with a problem up ahead that I am crapping myself enough about as it is? If Alexander were not my brother and I

Making his mark: Thomas tops out on
the first ascent of Raunachtstanz

to be much point dragging it all up there with me.
It would just be unnecessary ballast.

So now here I am, exactly where I wanted to
be. This is what I have always dreamed about –
new land, virgin rock, ahead of me nothing but
uncertainty. I take another deep breath and get
myself used to the idea that, for the next half hour,
I will have to give it everything I have got. The only
things that counts now, and the thing that will
dominate everything, is the little ledge 30 metres
above me. The first ten metres from the terrace are
easier than expected. A more or less illusory piece

◆ "DO NOT FALL!"

of protection, a Friend, resting on two cams flat in
the fluting, provides only a little security but at
least it calms the nerves. Until now retreat is still
an option, as I could reverse all the moves up to
this point. I am still in the green light zone. Ahead
of me, the wall steepens, the next few metres up to
a little depression look hard – after that, retreat
back down to the broad terrace will be cut off. I
can only hope that the continuation will not be
too hard. Hope? The way things look up there,
there can be no promise that things will get any
easier. A hidden hold, invisible from where I am
now standing, and everything would be resolved in
a series of harmonious moves. But who can give
me such a guarantee? It is a 50/50 game, heads or
tails, all or nothing – and I would sooner not shade
in the details if it turns out to be 'nothing'.

I can still quit the game at this point, be
reasonable, climb back down to the safety of the
terrace and enjoy the afternoon sun, but that, too,
would be 'nothing', absolutely nothing at all.

So I go for it, trying not to think about what
could happen. Place the rock boots precisely on
the sloping foot holds, reach in control to get the
thin side-pull in the fluting exactly right. I forget
everything around me, registering neither the sun
nor the blue sky. I no longer think about the
tempting grass cushion on the terrace below, as
everything inside me concentrates on the quality
of my next moves. And they are getting sketchier:
my body starts to shake slightly, I can no longer
place my boots quite as precisely on the smears.
Two rather dubious moves on tiny side-pulls and
I can bridge across the shallow depression. After
six metres of climbing, consistently at my limit,
the first physical rest arrives but, as yet, there is
still no respite for the psyche – the questionable
protection is a long way below me, there is no way

were not responsible for the little dwarf I would
send him up there on the lead – that would sort
out the nonsense in his head. Why can't I be as
calm as him?

I sort out the gear on my harness. I don't need
much – a 3 and a 3 ½ Friend and three small
knifeblades. This is actually far too little for a pitch
in this price range, definitely a grade VII, but since
the other gear will not go in, there does not seem

it would hold a fall. That is one thing I can not afford to do. If I take off from here I would thunder onto the terrace next to Alexander. . .

The moves that lie above me have a far from calming influence; on the contrary, they make me even more nervous. It all looks pretty smooth. I need to get a good bit of gear in, now! Feverishly, I weigh up the options. I discover a narrow crack behind a little sod of grass and stick a knife-blade in it. Two careful blows with the hammer and, tzzzing, both the peg and the flake fly off the wall in a high arc.

I curse, swear, beg somebody or some thing, even a loving God, for a some kind of protection but nothing, nothing goes in, the rock is too compact, no peg, no Friend, no nut. Retreat is cut off. I could cry. Even the most carefully chosen curse is no help at all here, pleading and begging are no use either, I am stuck in a one way street with the arrow on the sign pointing upwards, I am pleading that it is not a dead end. There is only one traffic rule here and it says 'Do not fall!' I know that I am the only real piece of protection, my fingers, my feet, my brain that commands them to do the right things – climb, grab hold, keep going. One mistake

OK, I'm pleased with you, well done. Oh, the little ledge, have a rest, I'm coming, be with you in a minute . . ."

The release of tension changes to a sudden feeling of nausea. I choke the last remains of doubt from my body and slowly risk a quick look down – what a crazy pitch!

Alexander follows the pitch; he has to make an effort but it does not stress him out. Leading and seconding are just two completely different things. He comes up to the stance, congratulates me and talks yet again about the possible first ascents over on the Birnhorn – is he off his head, or what? Thank God there are only two obviously easier pitches to go.

Topping out, we clap each other on the shoulders, congratulating ourselves on our first first ascent, our new line through new territory. We have turned the uncertainty of this line into a thing of certainty, the essence of which can be captured in words: eight pitches of best quality rock, grade VII, very bold and demanding slab climbing. We even have a name for it: 'Raunachtstanz'.

We abseil off and hike back down to the valley, absolutely full of it now, the words come tumbling

◆ A WILD THOUGHT RACES THROUGH MY HEAD:
"MAN, I CAN DO THIS!"

33

and I will be lying next to Alexander, 20 metres below, a thought I can not allow myself to dwell on and must dismiss now. The cards have been newly shuffled, a new game is about to start, and I know it is a game I must not lose.

Right then. This is the way I wanted it. I arrange my fingers on an edge that is hardly there and hold this position. A wild thought races through my head: "Man, I can do this!" Intuitively, my body starts the correct sequence of moves, I latch one edge after another, a sequence of fast, dynamic moves. It is as if I were an outside observer, who is merely spectating and has no further influence on the action. "Not bad, Thomas!" he says, "That was

out as we verbally reclimb the slabs, happy as a pair of little scallywags after playing a successful trick. Down on the road, we stick out our thumbs and get a lift into Traunstein. It is Friday evening and the young climbers are all in the pub. We really should be getting off home but can not resist bursting into the pub and telling them all about our new route adventures. At ten o' clock we phone Mother; she has been worried and comes to pick us up. To put her mind at rest we report back to her about a lovely Grade V – "It just took a while, that's all" – and, like the good boys we are, thank her once again for giving us the early morning taxi ride.

Mother Huber in the Hoher Tauern.
Even if her enthusiasm for rock climbing is limited, she still shares
the family's wholehearted passion for mountaineering

34

to a few insiders but not to the broad spectrum of mountain enthusiasts.

In those days the scene was shaped by mountaineers in the classic mould who put their efforts into mastering the great walls in the Alps and perhaps going on an expedition once in their lives. Routes such as the North Face of the Eiger, the Bonatti Pillar on the Drus or the Tre Cime Direttissimas were frequently repeated and the classic 'sixes' scattered across the Dachstein, the Dolomites and the Karwendel were all the rage. Many people climbed using Walter Pause's list of one hundred routes in On Extreme Rock as their guide and everyone went on the ice. Specialists did not count for much.

Was there anyone in those days who did not compete for the first winter ascent of the Solleder Route or the first solo ascent of the Walker Spur? Anyone who had completed the three great North Walls belonged to a circle of the 'greatest' among 'extreme' climbers. For a whole decade The North Face of the Droites was considered to be the most difficult mixed route, the Philipp Flamm dihedral on the Civetta as the boldest free climbing in the Alps and the Central Pillar of Freney as the ultimate challenge on the granite of Mont Blanc.

Thomas Huber senior, Alexander and Thomas' father, belonged in those days to that élite circle of extremists who climbed on the rock and the ice, the limestone of the Eastern Alps and the granite of the Western Alps, with their big boots, fiffi hooks and bivvy bags, always on the look out for 'adventure' and a few partners who were prepared to go that one step further.

Reinhold Messner

After the Age of the Direttissima and the conquering of all the eight thousanders, mountaineering in central Europe lost its perspective. Vague information about a new wave of free climbing in America's Yosemite National Park and expeditions on the six and seven thousanders which had gone tragically wrong were of interest

» My brother Günther died aged 24 on Nanga Parbat and it was only by good fortune that I survived. Our common dreams were shattered by this event. After dozens of joint first ascents and perhaps a thousand routes climbed as a rope of two from one moment to the next I was alone. There were so many things we could still have achieved together! My mountaineering life would have been different together with Günther. Our joint creativity, energy and experience were worth more than the sum total of the parts. Of course, there had been rivalry between us, too, and as the older brother it went without saying that, on the rock, I should take the lead. But Günther was always there trying to overtake me, and he had already waved goodbye to his civilian profession before we went to Nanga Parbat. Thomas and Alexander Huber have survived their years of *sturm and drang*. They are a team, a rope, a pair of brothers with enormous potential. R.M. «

Perhaps, as Walter Bonatti writes, this short in-between era, after conquering the highest and before discovering the smallest mountains in the world, signified the end of the classic age of mountaineering. Nevertheless, it was an exciting time and mountaineering was dangerous. Only later did the specialists arrive, together with new safety equipment, climbing competitions and commercial expeditions to the summit of Mount Everest.

After thirty years of improvement – better equipment, more scientific and specific training methods, worldwide comparibility – a return to classic mountaineering seems probable. The highest level of difficulty on the highest mountains of the world can once more be united with a clean style of climbing. Just imagine it: The Huber brothers climb the concave West Face of Makalu directly to the summit of this eight thousander, in alpine style, free climbing for the most part, descent via the normal route . . .   R.M.

Father Huber, with the protection methods used in his day, on the Direct South Arête on the 3rd Watzmannkind

On the Breithorn in the Valais. The boys' father trusted his sons in the mountains from an early age. In just 3 years they did more than 30 four-thousanders in the Alps

Alexander at 11

Thomas at 13

THE END OF SILENCE

THE 11TH GRADE IN THE MOUNTAINS

On the crux pitch (X+) of 'End of Silence' on the
North Face of the Feuerhörndl,
Berchtesgaden/Germany, 1984
Thomas Huber

I am eighteen and my enthusiasm for climbing is
boundless, bordering on fanaticism. It makes it all
the more difficult to do anything I am not totally
motivated to do. The daily trip to school is
something I feel to be total harassment. For me
school is a necessary evil; it robs me of my free time
and gets in the way of my climbing. My ambition is
focused on other goals, I detest logarithms and
citric acid and Sallust is a matter of complete
indifference to me, even if my teacher can muster
no understanding for this whatsoever. My marks
suffer accordingly. This time, they were again just
about good enough for entry into the next class up.
I work on the minimalist principle, no more. In
Latin lessons I read climbing magazines and draw
topos of the routes I have done.
Unfortunately for me there are some days when
the teachers will not tolerate a moment's
inattention. Six lessons of enforced concentration

become a marathon of suffering, as the second hand on my watch refuses to be influenced by my impatience, creeping forward at the same slow, ponderous rate. Sixty times and a minute has passed, the whole thing sixty times means only one hour and at least five full hours equal one school day. Calculated in terms of seconds, the watch has to tick 18,000 times before I am released from the suffering. Such thoughts tear me apart inside. I feel like a time bomb, ready to explode, waiting as the last of these 18,000 seconds are counted down. Then I let loose my energy, the colour returns to my cheeks, my lethargy is blown away and life can begin.

Out of the claustrophobia of the school buildings, I toss the tatty old school bag onto the back seat of

◆ "THIS IS NOT A RED DOT"

the car and head off to Karlstein to live the free life again at last. I know every bend on this stretch of road so Alexander and I get to the crags at Bad Reichenhall pretty fast. The crags themselves are barely higher than 20 metres. This was the training area used by our 'alpine' fathers, rusty pitons are the relics of their routes, which they climbed using every technical trick in the book to prepare themselves for their great alpine undertakings. It is in this historic open-air training facility that we find our new challenge – to climb the old routes with no artificial aid. There are also plenty of

opportunities here to do new routes. It is an exciting adventure playground for a handful of nutcases mad about climbing.

The importance of this place in our climbing lives cannot be ignored, as sport climbing becomes increasingly the focus for our skills. To begin with we climbed only on alpine terrain, the local crag being nothing more than a natural training venue

where we could get a better grasp of what was required on the big faces. Over the years, however, this attitude changed and as climbing at the absolute limit of one's ability became increasingly important we spent more and more of our free afternoons and weekends at Karlstein.

In the mountains the psychological factor is mostly far too dominant for a significant improvement in performance to be achieved. There, we do climbs that are basically well within our capabilities, anything else would be too risky. For up on the big alpine faces one cannot risk taking a fall, due to the questionable nature of the protection. Compare this with the local crag, where conditions are absolutely ideal; the customary good bolt protection means that the performance-inhibiting psychological factors shrink to almost nothing and it is correspondingly easy for us to shift our performance curve upwards. In those days, our calculation was a very simple one: well protected route = increased willingness to take a fall, level of difficulty of climbing = personal performance level X. Applying classic school mathematics to the solution of this equation, my personal performance level X would be the result of multiplying the level of difficulty of the climbing by the increased willingness to take a fall, divided by the protection factor. Stupid? Of course – this is the logical proof that climbing and school simply do not go together. In any case, climbing is much more a product of logic than of dialectics – you estimate whether something will go or not and if it will not go you have to investigate the causes. Climbers do not need equations; we have our own rules. They are defined by the right feeling for the rock, by the intuition and the mental strength demanded by the hard routes.

More and more, climbing has lost the nimbus of a heroic act and recently has been more akin to a gymnastic routine. The ladders and etriers, still used only a short time ago, are now rotting in a box in the gear cellar and it was only as a last resort on an alpine first ascent that they were last put to questionable use. They have been replaced by pure muscle power and technique, the specialist rubber on the rock shoes and the gymnasts' chalk are the only acceptable 'technical aids' nowadays. Ultimately, a little red point became the model and the motif for our climbing philosophy.

'Redpoint' is in fact just a small red dot painted on the rock at the start of a route that has been

The North Face of the Feuerhörndl,
Bershtesgaden Alps

Systematic training brings success
on Weiße Rose, XI/8c+, Schleierwasserfall, Tirol

climbing. The first route in the lower tenth grade (X-) was climbed by Englishman Jerry Moffat in 1983 but from then on it was Wolfgang Güllich who kept tight hold of the reins; indeed, for a time it seemed that he alone was responsible for further advances in difficulty. Kanal im Rücken (X), Punks in the Gym (X+), Wallstreet (XI-) and finally the famed and fabled Action Directe (XI) were the first routes of their standard in the world.

It was not by accident that Wolfgang Güllich was the main protagonist in the pursuit of the highest levels of difficulty in sport climbing. He was one of the first to apply the systematic training methods used in other highly developed performance sports to climbing. Without professional training the 11th grade can not be achieved. Nowadays sport climbing is a performance sport and there is no other branch of mountaineering where this is applied in such a pure form.

Eleventh grade sport climbing – this is a sport with extremely high physical and psychological demands. Only with a very well-trained set of muscles are you able to solve the extremely difficult move sequences involved. The necessary techniques could only be developed as a result of huge increases in power. The route Om, for example, first climbed by Alexander Huber in 1992, involves extremely dynamic climbing. A maximum distance between holds of 1.80 metres requires the climber to execute a 'deadpoint' move or 'dyno': using both arms, the body is propelled upwards, enabling the climber to catch the next hold with one hand at exactly that point where upward movement is still occurring and before the body begins to decelerate and fall.

In 1991 Wolfgang Güllich introduced the eleventh grade (XI) to climbing with his ascent of Action Directe. This was without doubt the hardest route of its kind in the world at the time and a defining moment in the rapid development of extreme sport

Without professional training the 11th grade cannot be achieved – sport climbing is a high-performance sport

Extreme body tension moves on the severely overhanging crux of Alexander's own route Resistance, XI–/8c, Schleierwasserfall

With the first ascent of La Rambla (XI/8c+) in the Spanish sport climbing area of Siurana, Alexander was assured of his place on the international climbing stage

Roof climbing: Alexander on his route Open Air,
XI/9a, Schleierwasserfall, Tirol

Alexander on the Segundo Salto of his route La Rambla,
XI/8c+, Siurana, Spain

climbed free. Perhaps the surrealist René Magritte would write below it "This is not a red dot" and he would be right, for the mark itself is formalistically entirely without meaning. It could be blue, yellow or green, a checked pattern or something else. What is significant is the idea behind the point, the intrinsic thoughts that reside within it. It is this splash of paint that embodies our climbing philosophy. Kurt Albert created it and with it he conquered the climbing world. To collect as many red points as possible is the ultimate goal of every climber; this is even taken to the extent that a route is only considered to have had a valid ascent when it has been 'redpointed'. The rules that derive from this red point are limited to three fundamental principles: climbing a route on the lead, climbing using only natural holds (i.e. free and using only pitons or bolts for protection) and climbing without falls from the bottom to the top in one push. There were times when the redpoint seemed to happen

Only the swear words bear any resemblance to normal speech. It is, however, typical of the climbing-specific cursing ritual that to a great extent it is your own ego that bears the brunt of the verbal abuse. Depending on the degree of sensitivity the scale extends from simply calling yourself a loser right up to grandiose accusations of inadequacy involving language of a more faecal nature. But it is important not to attach too much importance to this. Once the redpoint candidate has arrived back on the ground after an unsuccessful attempt the anger soon subsides. You focus on the next attempt or shift the blame for the failure onto the way the wind was blowing, for example.

After an afternoon's climbing at Karlstein, whether successful or not, we pack our rucksacks and head across a meadow a few steps to the Kugelbachbauer, a mountain inn right next door to the crag. This inn has almost become our second home; the innkeeper Heidi knows our predilection

◆ THERE WERE TIMES WHEN THE REDPOINT SEEMED TO HAPPEN FOR US AS IF BY MAGIC

for us as if by magic and others, often enough, when it took us days to get the redpoint. Generally we were climbing at our absolute limit. First we had to split the route up into individual moves and work out each move separately, 'bouldering out' the route. Subsequently we co-ordinated the individual moves, practising the sequences long enough to feel we had a chance of linking the whole route together in one push. At some stage or other, and with a little help from the Holy Ghost, a successful redpoint ascent was then made.

A redpoint can be defined further; indeed, it requires further clarification. Success on the first attempt, with no previous knowledge of the route, receives the accolade 'on sight', the same thing but with prior information is called a 'flash' and if success comes only after several attempts, or even days spent working the route, it is known as a 'normal' redpoint ascent. In the sport of climbing everything has its own specific name, every task, every shape of hold, every climbing situation, every article of equipment. The resultant climbers' jargon is difficult for the layman to understand; he would be hopelessly lost with a piece of advice like "Hey, you up there, crimp the little sidepull with your right and get the toehook with your left and you won't barndoor!"

for sweet things and often keep the cakes she has not managed to sell during the day for us. Life can be so good. The irritation of the morning's lessons and the afternoon's failed redpoint attempts forgotten, we sit in the evening sun with a mug of banana buttermilk and a piece of apple pie – jumbo size, huge portion of whipped cream – engrossed in tales and lengthy explanations of complicated hold sequences. Finally, when all the cruxes have been climbed at the garden table, each of us dreams of redpointing his own current project. How is there supposed to be enough room in my head for all the school stuff they are force-feeding me as well?

The first ascent of Jenseits von Eden (East of Eden) at Karlstein is my first IX. It represents a step into a new area of difficulty and is made possible by my unbroken ambition. If I were to apply this degree of enthusiasm and industriousness to school I would certainly average straight As. To transfer the limit of your performance from the local crag to the mountains is like an examination for the master craftsman's diploma for it is only then that you can be sure you really have mastered the newly achieved grade. Once the mountaineering élite starts talking about the ninth grade in the mountains and Wolfgang

Müller sets the standards with his route Odyssee in the Kaisergebirge there is no stopping us. The only question is on which face 'our' IX might be lurking. Criteria number one states that no obvious line should be discernable; the more featureless and compact the face, the better suited it is to our project. Secondly, the face should on first impressions appear to be so impossible that nobody would normally think of climbing it. I undertake some general research by studying the

looks hellishly difficult, but it does look as if there might be a solution. Above this, however, everything looks very different with vaguer features leading to a very smooth summit wall that is another 150 metres in height. The only logical line is a grey, overhanging pillar sandwiched between the two yellow precipices on the upper third of the face. From a distance this section looks absurd, unclimbable. But that is exactly what fires us with such enthusiasm – to get to grips

◆ THIS NORTH FACE IS EXACTLY WHAT WE ARE LOOKING FOR: STEEP, COMPACT, IMPOSSIBLE!

Berchtesgaden guidebook, searching for the face with the hardest and fiercest aid routes. Three walls in the Berchtesgaden area make it onto the shortlist: the South Face of the Untersberg, the South Face of the Kleines Mühlsturzhorn and the North Face of the Feuerhörndl.

The South Face of the Untersberg really does look frighteningly impressive but on closer inspection the rock on our intended route seems too loose. The South Face of the Kleines Mühlsturzhorn is quite a passable alternative but what we do not fancy at all is the time-consuming uphill grind to the foot of the cliff. That leaves the North Face of the Feuerhörndl on the Reiteralm.

A short while later Alexander and I climb the neighbouring north buttress of Hirscheck to get a better look at our new line. For the first time we can view 'our' face from a new angle. We are speechless. This North Face is exactly what we are

looking for: steep, compact, impossible! So far Werner Schertle has been the only one to accept the challenge of this wall, using every trick in the book to aid his way through the overhangs. His line is unique, and awesomely impressive, but the yellow rock looks to be very brittle in parts and far from ideal from a free climbing point of view.

But 50 metres to the left of the Schertle Route, grey compact rock predominates. Up to half height, the line of the route is defined by a prominent groove system with roofs and steep face climbing. It all

with something which conventional wisdom would dismiss as absurd. In this way our grade IX in the mountains will be an all-determining challenge.

Alexander and I are totally fascinated by this 350 metres of madness; we are mad for it, cannot wait to set off up this wall. For us, the only thing that exists any more is the North Face of the Feuerhörndl and the only thing preventing us from mounting a premature attempt are the many unanswered questions between the start and the top. We must study the wall in more detail and first make sketch of it so we are not wandering about the featureless vertical face without a plan.

I have just started doing a photography course at school. We have been learning how to develop film and use the darkroom to transfer images to photographic paper. The teacher sets us the task of photographing an aspect of nature. This is the solution to our wall problem and finally I can combine homework with something useful! Working in the darkroom gives me the opportunity to enlarge shots of specific details of the face, enabling us to study the structure of the rock more closely. While my school mates take photographs of trees, lakes and reeds I try to capture every detail of the face with my camera. The results of my work in the darkroom look just about perfect to me. What had once seemed impossible now has a touch of the tangible about it, even if it does still look every bit as audacious and presumptuous as before.

When I present the set of shots to my teacher he does not really know where to begin with them. He is a mountaineer himself and he knew I was wanting to photograph mountains but had expected moods and panoramas, the kind of motifs you find on a calendar. For him, my pictures are a grey soup devoid of any kind of excitement. I

Alexander abseils off End of Silence frustrated
after the first, unsuccessful, attempt

End of Silence, Part 1: Alexander and Thomas top out. The first ascent is in the bag, the redpoint still awaits

try to explain to him that that is exactly what my pictures set out to do, and that the excitement only arises when one gives serious thought to these shades of grey, that then images appear within the image, faces and forms, line and structure, for the photo is not a bold and simple visual representation but a vehicle for inspiration of a new visual world. He can only shake his head at this theory. But I refuse to be beaten; this is all about getting a good mark, something I urgently need in order to improve my overall average. I illustrate the phenomenon of an untouched world, one that can be seen but which no man has so far set foot in; at the same time I enthuse about my idea of drawing a line on this series of pictures that will make the irrational into a rational world capable of being experienced. Unfortunately my

just as uninteresting for me as the pitying looks of my school mates, who just label me as crazy. Let them keep and cherish their perspectives, they are of no interest to me; the reality I seek to realize looks different, and they will never comprehend it. Only Alexander sees the logic of this challenge; namely, to reach the highest point of the North Face of the Feuerhörndl by the most impossible looking line. Our common sense says yes and thus the summit becomes the absolute goal where all the threads of our actions converge.

A first ascent on a mountain crag – that means adrenaline in the blood. Uncertainty cramps the otherwise smooth and harmonious moves you make, causing them to appear hesitant and shaky. Gone are the pleasant weekend trips to the local

◆ THE TENSION BUILDS TO A CLIMAX

teacher is not receptive to this representation, he still sees only grey on grey. As a positive example of a picture that is charged with emotion and therefore successful he shows me two ducks flying over the Chiemsee lake. It becomes obvious that he cannot follow my thought processes and we are both steadfastly talking at cross purposes.

In the end the poor marks for photography are

crag; no time for banana buttermilk at the Kugelbachbauer. We are working on another building site now and it is deep in shadows and more adventurous than anything before.

The start of the route is at a small ledge with solid grass upholstery. The wall starts at the right hand corner and grows 350 metres up into the milky blue sky. We are both nervous and actually ask

ourselves what we are doing here. No one has forced us into it, it is all purely voluntary . . . is this supposed to be fun? The answer – a definite "no". So why are we here then? Maybe we are idiots with serious behavioural problems. We are searching and do not know what we are searching for. Let's go swimming at the Thumsee, we are bound to see someone there . . .

Alexander looks at the watch and comments tersely that it is about time to get started. Putting an end to all the analysis, he hammers in two pegs and hands me the whole rack. I arrange it on my harness, lace up my rock boots and lean back a little, craning my neck to get a look at the wall above me. The crippling questions about the sense of it all are forgotten now. I know exactly what I am going to find – new territory – and what I want – I want to set foot on it, commit myself to this adventure, reach the goal by the line we have envisaged.

It is much harder than we imagined. We have to fight for every metre, feeling our way into virgin territory and experiencing both positive and negative surprises. Something that looks like a very small edge from below turns out to be a hold you can get your whole hand around, while a section of face climbing that on first appearances seems easy actually becomes a serious problem. It is certainly not boring. We take several falls working the various hard face sequences and more than once find ourselves a good six metres out from the last piece of gear.

The tension builds to a climax. We feel out little edges and rugosities and place a suitable skyhook, to hold ourselves temporarily in position and free our hands to place a bolt. The next few seconds are crucial, all our senses concentrated on one square centimetre. Slowly weight the skyhook, calmly take a deep breath and observe carefully – is the point of the skyhook slipping out of the nick in the rock? Will the edge snap under the load concentrated on a single point? Or is everything quiet and stable?

"Pliiing!"

The noise of the skyhook ripping out under the load is the starting signal for a rollercoaster ride. There is nothing else for it but to repeat the process as often as necessary until the thing eventually holds. Then, working in a generally uncomfortable and cramped position, we hammer a hole for the bolt using a hand-held drill bit. For at least 20 minutes I thrash away with the hammer and drill bit until the star drill sinks into

48

... the fear of once more being just about to achieve success, of being close enough to reach out and grab it – only to fail yet again one metre before the finishing line. I have linked the first 99 moves of the route (Open Air, XI, 9a) 20 times with no falls, forcing myself to get back on it after failing on the 100th move for the 20th time. The dyno to the next hold is huge and the finger pocket I am aiming for is pretty small and hard to latch. Again and again I hit the lip of the pocket; I am starting to doubt whether I will get it next go. Why should next time be any different? As I set up for the jump my strength is nearly gone and the hold is so small I can hardly see it from where I am. But if I allow this pattern of thought to spiral out of control I will never do the route. There is only one path to success: self-belief. The belief that I am capable of doing it!

I am in the right position now to make the dyno. First I have to crouch down into it in order to give myself more distance over which to propel my body. I now no longer need to think; in fact it is out of the question – all the muscles in my body have to give 100% now. The move has been worked to perfection; defying gravity, the body arches upwards like a wave, the left hand lashing out at double the speed to latch the hold I am aiming for. Reaching deadpoint state I cram my fingers into the pocket – two fingers, the tips only – as the extreme pressure builds and my fingers bite into the rock. For a brief moment the body remains motionless and I pull as hard as I can, almost blacking out from the strain. On the 21st attempt I latch that pocket and stay in contact with the rock, open my eyes, position my left foot and pull through to the first good hold.   A. H.

IF I ALLOW THIS PATTERN OF THOUGHT TO SPIRAL OUT OF CONTROL I WILL NEVER DO THE ROUTE

The crux move on Open Air, XI/9a is described by Alexander "... defying gravity the body arches upwards like a wave, the left hand lashing out at double the speed to latch the hold I am aiming for"

the rock. Then blow out the bore hole, sleeve in, hammer in the bolt – done, finished. Finished placing the bolt, reserves of strength finished and filthy from head to toe. This combination of climbing, tension and drilling takes so much strength that we swop leads after three bolts, which corresponds to about 15 metres of new ground. After five pitches we realize that we are not up to the route. What lies behind us is nothing in comparison to what is rearing its ugly head up above.

◆ WE GET THE DEVASTATING FEELING THAT WE ARE FAILURES

We get the devastating feeling that we are failures. We are demoralized, pull long faces and admit to each other that we still have a long way to go before we are up to climbing this line. We go back down to the deck and look up at the headwall again; it seems absolutely impossible now. As we hike back down to the valley and get our feet firmly back on the ground, viewing the facts for what they are, a little spark of hope appears in the fire we had almost quenched – wasn't there a little edge three metres above me that led into a shallow groove? At this moment it becomes clear that we are going to come back. But before we do we have got a lot of work to do. We have to get better; and this line is incentive enough . . .

Two years later we are back at the end of the fifth pitch, the point we retreated from. A lot has changed since then. We are now into easy grade X, Alexander's biceps have taken on enormous proportions and we have a keener eye for the logical line on a first ascent. On ground where, two years ago, we did not dare to climb any further we now lock off on the tiniest crimps and intinctively seem to always find a way of climbing out of impossible looking situations. The only thing that has remained the same is the uneasy feeling we get when placing a skyhook. We weight it with the same care and the same feeling of suspense and we still take a deep breath when all goes well.

Unlike the first attempt, this time I haul a battery-powered drill up on a tag line. Press the start button, press the machine and drill bit against the rock, blow out the hole, hammer in the bolt sleeve, tighten the hanger with a No. 7 spanner – all done and dusted in two minutes flat. What a hassle it was when we needed 20 minutes thrashing about with the hand drill and then had hardly any strength left for the climbing. This eminently strength-saving device allows us to do harder moves between the bolts and place them further apart as well.

As we place the last bolt and, a little later, top out on the summit plateau, we have reached the end of our common journey. A broad grin and the mutual congratulations on our success and our first ascent is finished, six years after I first saw the wall, studied the black and white photographs and discovered the line. Up to today it was something fictitious; only Alexander and I knew the route and saw the indistinct features that led us onwards to our goal. Now this line is a reality and visible to all-comers; the bolts point the way like signposts up the whole route and the topo provides important additional information.

Our initial idea of an alpine grade IX has become a straight X with a big fat question mark hanging over a section on the tenth pitch that we were not able to free climb. We got past this featureless bit of the wall with two bolts placed one above the other; it was not possible any other way. But we know that this bit will also go free even if it is too hard for us right now. We suspect that it will mean a step across the grade X line. But there is no end without a beginning. Alexander is planning to do a grade XI sport climb this year. For me, the presumed end of the route on the Feuerhörndl is, at the same time, the beginning of a new challenge.

The crux sequence of End of Silence . . .

We have both chosen the directions we want to go in; further research into the inner workings of this line will be my problem in the future. From a 300-metre mosaic consisting of pockets, crimps, flat edges and cracks a single unit of free-flowing, linked sequences of moves will arise. At the present it is still in a raw state, the fine-tuning is still missing. The last brush strokes, certainly the hardest to apply, will lend the completed work of art its uniqueness – and this work of art is entitled 'redpoint in a single day'.

The path that leads there is a long one, and it involves a whole lot of work. I organize myself so that I am not dependent any anyone; working out the ideal sequence would really tax the patience of any climbing partner. I hang a static rope down the top half of the route and build myself a little oasis of calm and relaxation in the middle of the steepest part of the face; one square metre of horizontal ledge made from a discarded cupboard door, held in place by a few slings.

I abseil down the wall and work the crux, protected only by an ascender. The ascender becomes by climbing partner; it is patient, attentive and does exactly what I want it to do. The more often I play around up there on the wall the more I get used to the idea of being alone. The initial fear of making a mistake and free-falling 300 metres to deck out on the rocks below gradually gives way to a feeling of absolute safety. Up here, I am free of all the inhibiting disturbances and with every move my goal gets nearer. I can feel myself getting stronger with every attempt. The sequence of moves, so jerky at first, is getting more rounded and harmonious. Every detail, every little unevenness in the rock, is etched on my memory and defines my movements – without realizing it, I am becoming a part of this wall. It is only now that the line I discovered all those years ago really takes over completely. From now on it rules everything – my deeds, my emotions, my whole life. I, who discovered this new territory for myself, have now become a slave to my own route. The grey rock discloses my own unknown characteristics; it lays

euphoria is relativized. Only now do I understand the actual crux of my redpoint idea; the first nine pitches are just the lead-in to the real route, which actually begins 200 metres above the ground right in the middle of the tenth pitch. In real terms, the size of this new problem boils down to four metres and eight moves. But the true dimension of these four metres calls everything else into question spatially. Compared to the whole route this section is laughably short but it grows to irrational proportions and at the moment of failure it becomes an insurmountable obstacle.

By now I am desperate. It is impossible for me to break through this barrier – my barrier. I know

I AM OBSESSED AND FASCINATED AT THE SAME TIME

that, purely theoretically, this redpoint idea is achievable and that the reason for my failure is not physical. What I lack is the ability to break through into a hitherto unknown mental level of climbing. It is not enough to have all the moves in my head. Even wanting it with every fibre of my body is not the key with which to unlock the secret of these four metres. It is the letting go of all emotion that is indispensable for success. Wanting success, fear of success, desire, even love and hate – it all has to be switched off. The mind has to be free to give the body only those impulses it requires to perform the moves accurately. Just four metres of rock . . .

15 August 1994. The weather report could not be better. Alexander agrees to hold my ropes the next day. Physically I am in top form; mentally I replay the four metres over and over again in my mind so that I know exactly what is required. The prerequisites are better than ever and at nine o'clock we are at the start of the route, ready and focused. I get to the rest point on the tenth pitch after five hours, as expected.

I wait for the right moment. Nothing else is important, nothing. The world is reduced to just eight moves. I shake out, have a dip in the chalk bag and start the countdown – three, two, one.

An hour later I sit amidst the blueberry bushes and mountain pines at the top of the route with Alexander. How many days and hours have I given for this moment; what had I done to be able to milk it for all it is worth? I had always known that this dream – a dream I started dreaming as an

bare something over which I have no influence. The direction I take is now determined by the line of my new route, my body just an instrument with which to conquer the new territory of my soul.

I am obsessed and fascinated at the same time. I am on that wall as often as I can. I have to solve its puzzle, working all the moves until they become automatic. Between attempts I recover on my board and stare down at a world that, in such moments, seems alien to me. I sit there in a state of splendid isolation like a piece of cheese under a transparent cheese dome, and I am satisfied, for here I have all the important things I need in my life – safety, security, harmony, challenge, a goal to aim for and respect. The only thing missing is love; that lives in another world . . .

After 20 days I reckon I am strong enough to go for the one-day redpoint. Together with Roman, a friend I have complete trust in, I make my first attempt. At first I am totally satisfied with my performance. I redpoint everything up to the ninth pitch – the difficulties are between VIII and X – and on the tenth pitch, the crux, I am only three metres away from a resounding success. When, on the second, third and fourth day of attempts, I keep falling off at the same place my initial

eighteen-year-old youth – was no hare-brained fantasy. I had always held on to the image of this moment, as if it were already reality, but could have no way of knowing when the moment would come.

So for the second time I find myself on the top of the Feuerhörndl with Alexander. I can now feel the power of the route waning, a power that had possessed me for years. In its place my dreams of new territory become more concrete. The End of Silence – down below, life awaits.

53

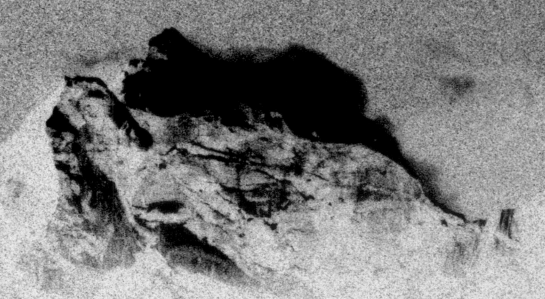

Reinhold Messner

Within one century the art of rock climbing has increased by seven degrees, from the fourth to the eleventh degree of difficulty. If we take into account the war years and the short periods of stagnation that means about one degree increase approximately every twelve years: V 1912, VI 1925, VII 1936, VIII 1968, IX 1980, X 1990, XI today.

Thus the development of the art of climbing has not been exponential and it has been accompanied by continuous improvements in equipment such as footwear and protection devices. It is only these continuing innovations in climbing aids, whether bolts or cliffhangers, that have managed to hold back the development of pure rock climbing.

In climbing and mountaineering there are no hard and fast rules, only the self-imposed limitations of the protagonists and the unspoken silent agreement, from generation to generation, as to where we all want to go. Of course, each generation is free to invent and use new methods of belaying and protection and the choice of route

also determines whether nuts, pitons or bolts are used to safeguard a stance. However, if we could all agree that climbing were to become a function of human ability rather than technological advances it would seem sensible, in order to preserve the mountains as a medium by which people can measure themselves, to limit the infrastructure to just a few pieces of protection and, where possible, to remove these after use.

It seems obvious that a new route on a blank rock face devoid of cracks will nowadays be protected by expansion bolts, but does this mean that routes, which were first climbed 75, 50 or 25 years ago without bolts, should now be climbed using modern equipment? No, for each route represents a period and in additional to the sporting element there are also the inherent emotional and historical dimensions to consider.

Although at the end of the last millennium the 'alpinism of deprivation' twice failed to achieve common currency, it is to this that the future belongs. Only with a reduction in the number of climbing aids and protection devices can the

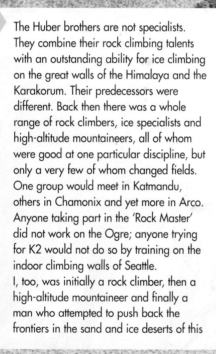

> The Huber brothers are not specialists. They combine their rock climbing talents with an outstanding ability for ice climbing on the great walls of the Himalaya and the Karakorum. Their predecessors were different. Back then there was a whole range of rock climbers, ice specialists and high-altitude mountaineers, all of whom were good at one particular discipline, but only a very few of whom changed fields. One group would meet in Katmandu, others in Chamonix and yet more in Arco. Anyone taking part in the 'Rock Master' did not work on the Ogre; anyone trying for K2 would not do so by training on the indoor climbing walls of Seattle.
> I, too, was initially a rock climber, then a high-altitude mountaineer and finally a man who attempted to push back the frontiers in the sand and ice deserts of this world. It is only because I have continued to change terrain as I grow older, that I have been able to continue to find new challenges in the vertical, high and horizontal wildernesses. For almost thirty years I have been able to push boundaries, break taboos, solve problems, be that on the Central Buttress of the Heiligkreuz in the Dolomites, without a mask on Mount Everest in the Himalaya or crossing Greenland diagonally lengthways. In order to solve the remaining problems, specialisms are no longer sufficient. Man with all his capabilities is once again challenged if he wants to set new standards. Each generation of pioneers will be overtaken by another generation every ten years, as in the times of Paul Preuß and Walter Bonatti. « R.M.

further development of post-modern mountaineering be continued *ad infinitum*. A process combining sections of old techno-routes to create a new free climbing route is one of the positive developments, in contrast to the banalization of the classics with bolts and all manner of tricks in order to make the great walls more and more 'user friendly'.

I myself have never placed a bolt, never used oxygen equipment and will never take a satellite telephone with me on an expedition. You see, out there at the end of the world – be that on the Eiger, the Ogre or K2 – the potential for discovery grows with the commitment, the difficulty, the effort and the exposure. If I hammer in bolts in order to overcome the most difficult sections, use oxygen equipment in order to reduce the struggle at high altitude, or use the satellite phone in order to keep in contact with civilisation then I am only deceiving myself.

At my age the mountains are 'getting bigger', and so I content myself these days with smaller, flatter objectives. But the Huber brothers have no sense of growing or shrinking mountains; for them and their kind there are plenty of new challenges: on an icefall in a gorge close to home or on the Colle de Speranza on Cerro Torre in Patagonia. Where there is no infrastructure, the mystery remains.

On the North West Ridge of Latok II, 7108 m, Karakorum/Pakistan, 1995
Alexander Huber

Ismail, our Base Camp cook, had brewed us coffee fit for a prince that afternoon. We had lingered over this, the last little luxury for a few days. Then, as the sun was setting and the heat was growing less intense, we made tracks.

The 'track' is a deadly irritating, five-kilometre-long pile of rubble leading to our Advance Base Camp on Latok II. Stones, stones, nothing but stones – sharp stones, rounded stones, big stones, little stones... Up and down we go, working our way across the moraines to our destination. How many times is this now? Today, however, it is different. We left Base Camp with a certain amount of celebration, for today, finally, the goal is

LATOK II
THE ART OF TURNING BACK

the summit and no longer the soul-destroying task of load-carrying in order to establish a tiny oasis amid the climatic rigours of extreme altitude. We waste no words on the coming days, but climb on into the night, each of us lost in thought, in a world of his own. We intend to climb through the night to avoid having to throw in the towel again due to the intense heat of the day. Mountains can be merciless.

About a week ago we climbed the ice wall to the broad col between Ogre II and Latok II. We had long since discarded our original objective, the vertical West Face of Latok II, as the stonefall in the West Face Couloir, the key to the route, was just too violent and unpredictable. The alternative was the North West Ridge. We wanted to climb the ice wall leading up to it at night. We hoped there would be less stonefall.

At first we were not especially worried that, despite the alpine start in the early hours of morning, we still had not quite reached the col. Later on, however, the strain was to tell even more as all at once we had to battle against an unimaginable heat. "We are off climbing on the high mountains of the world and it's freezing cold up there," or so we thought. We were not yet really aware of the fact that an increase in altitude in no way necessarily causes a fall in temperature. In the Himalayas, an increase in altitude is far more likely to produce a corresponding increase in temperature differentials. Biting cold during the night is followed by daytime sunlight that, when the wind drops, burns every last drop of sense from your head as the mountain forces you to your knees. Burnt out, drained and completely at the end of our tether we had to turn back after reaching the col, before we had really got going.

But we had learned from the experience. This time around, all six of us reach the pre-prepared and stocked camp at 5600 metres at the start of the North West Ridge of Latok II early, as the sun is rising. We are not intending to continue until the next morning. Thanks to the preplaced camps it has been a Sunday morning stroll up to here but from tomorrow onwards it's all Alpine Style, since the stretch that lies ahead has neither fixed ropes nor depots or camps in place. Everything we are likely to need over the next few days has now to be

The West Face of Latok II. Clearly visible to the left is the North West Ridge, the prominent tower at two-thirds height

carried with us. Too much weight reduces the chances of success, for now speed is of the essence, so we keep things to a minimum, packing only those items essential to sustain life. But what is essential? Back home it is the breakfast pot of coffee, up here on the mountain it is the insulated sleeping mat and a down sleeping bag for the night. We agree to dispense with tents, since we are expecting consistent difficulties on the extremely steep and rocky ridge and cannot afford any additional weight in our rucksacks.

To sleep beneath the heavens with no roof over your head is the dream of many a climber, but at an altitude of 6500 metres it is rather an uncompromising way to get to the summit. On this

◆ SUCH AN UNDERTAKING ALWAYS HAS CERTAIN SADO-MASOCHISTIC CHARACTERISTICS

exposed ridge we cannot be certain of finding sufficient snow to build a snow-cave and with this Alpine style of climbing it is also impossible to wait out a period of poor weather. We really will just have to trust to instinct, 'follow our noses' and try to make the right decisions as we go.

In the afternoon Hans and Jochen are again plagued by restlessness. They want to set off and prepare the route, climbing the first steep section today to enable us to get moving faster tomorrow. All four of us stretch out in the warm afternoon sun as the pair of them battle their way up the cold North side of the steep ridge section. Jochen struggles for a whole hour to break through a cornice. Finally there is no more time left to look for a suitable place to sleep for the night and they have to hack out a little platform in the steep ice slope.

We, on the other hand, have lots of room and with only four of us instead of six it is very comfortable in the warm tent. While the others wish the night away, we curse every forward movement of the hands of our watches. It is not that we have suddenly become aware of the abnormality of our act, voluntarily subjecting ourselves to the ravages of cold, heat, pain and hunger. We were clear about all that a long time ago. Such an undertaking always has certain sado-masochistic characteristics. We set about the mountain armed with pitons, ice axes and crampons and it retaliates by torturing us with reduced oxygen intake, stonefall, avalanche, wind, weather and other nastiness. And this is exactly what we want

Greetings from Yosemite

Alexander in the 'Squeezer' at 6300 metres

– we even need it! We are looking for just this kind of challenge and are prepared to put up with a load of stress to get it. But the uncertainty about what is to come drags at the nerves and is the real reason for the refusal to stare the passage of time straight in the face.

A brief look out of the tent fails to provide a solution. The weather looks settled; there is no reason to stay. We are driving up a one-way street, the direction of travel predetermined: "Follow the North West Ridge to the summit of Latok II!"

"What have I let myself in for here, then?" The thought runs through my head during breakfast. I could describe the fact that I am sitting here as the result of a chain of unfortunate circumstances. I

59

remember thinking, when leafing through Shirahata's Karakorum picture book, "That's the sort of wall we want!" I neither knew what the mountain was called, nor how high it was or where it lay. I simply registered the fact that it was pretty, and looked pretty damned hard too. Latok II, 7108 Meter high, central Karakorum, Pakistan, first climbed in 1977 by an Italian team via the South Ridge. And now I had to get up there too! We reached Hans and Jochen's bivouac site at sunrise. Like two little piles of human misery they were hanging from their ice screws rather than sitting on their ice ledge. If they had known in

◆ "WHAT HAVE I LET MYSELF IN FOR HERE, THEN?"

advance what kind of night was awaiting them they probably would not have gone for this open-air crash course in self-knowledge! As for us; well, we'd been climbing so we were too warm rather than too cold and the coming night still lay a long way ahead of us. This is the scheme that repeats itself *ad infinitum*, by which the

mountaineer constantly deceives himself. It is only possible to look the unpleasantness square in the eye by suppressing all the adverse accompanying symptoms. You view it all with rose-tinted spectacles, through which everything appears bathed in a more tolerable light. The only danger here is that idleness, weariness or a dulled perspective will rapidly cause you to lose the sharp focus required for critical situations and important decisions.

For the next three hours Jan breaks trail up the steep – 60 degrees in places – snow and ice slopes to the next barrier with the seriously difficult rock pitches. In the late afternoon I finally stand beneath a 50-metre high, slightly overhanging groove. A crack runs up the back, of a width which always worries climbers – a 'squeezer', as the Americans fondly refer to these dreaded off-width cracks. Although I know how badly protected these monster cracks are I decide to free climb the 'squeezer' rather than get involved in a lot of awkward techno stuff up one of the neighbouring hairline cracks. To begin with, I even manage to get some gear in to the left of the crack but eventually there is nothing else for it but to fight my way up the chimney for 15 unprotected metres. Such off-widths used to sap my strength even back in Yosemite, but here, at 6300 metres on Latok II, thrutching up a crack like this really does take my breath away. Lungs pumping, I hang like a ladybird in the crack, gasping for breath and trying to find the right tactics to effect upward progress. In order to shuffle up this filthy chasm I first have to squash all the air out of my lungs – only then can I squeeze my ribcage into and up the narrow slit. It takes a while before I hit on the right technique: jam myself into the crack, hyperventilate and then, before the next breathing crisis sets in, spend a few seconds nudging up a little higher, inch by inch. A Sisyphean task!

which the next man up is bringing with him. It seems to take forever until Hans finally appears – without my rucksack. He had to leave it halfway up the overhanging pitch. At this altitude, working your way up the rope on jumar clamps with two sacks is a real thrash, and one which Hans was not entirely keen on devoting himself to. For me this meant another half-hour wait, hoping that Jochen, the next man up, would bring up the gear.

I am now frozen stiff. As the last rays of sun disappear the expected drop in temperature sets in. Within minutes the mountain makes it clear who is calling the shots up here. The wind has dropped but even so I still can not imagine surviving the night without any equipment. Hans is already sitting up in his sleeping bag and he

The view across the sea of clouds of the Karakorum towards Tibet – and the front of bad weather closing in

Just a few minutes before sunset I reach a notch. It marks the end of this steep step and is at the same time an ideal spot to bivi. Down at Base Camp night has already fallen; I am catching the last rays of sun up here. Then the cold creeps up towards me too. Wearing thin fleece clothing and rock boots I stand in the notch and wait for my gear,

gives me his jacket and boots. At last, my sleeping bag arrives as well. The soup is warming and slowly warmth returns, while one pitch below the others stand around with little protection from the bitter cold. Only three hours later does Winni, the last man on the rope, arrive at the bivi ledge, totally wasted from waiting around for hours on end. It is too late now for a proper evening meal, so he promptly disappears into his sleeping bag. This is 'Alpine style' – live and unedited. By day you curse the too-heavy rucksack, by night you bemoan the fact that there is too little gear.

There is no wind at all. In spite of this we still shiver the endless night away beneath the stars, with the ever-present thought that the weather might turn. The barricade we have erected with

Time consuming: mixed ground on the North West Ridge

the meagre equipment to protect ourselves from such an eventuality is parchment-thin. We would not survive even a few days of hellish weather, not with our equipment and on such an exposed ridge. We sleep a little and think a lot.

The next morning there is a bit of a delay before the first of us starts cooking. Winni is not feeling particularly good. The hours of waiting around in the cold, the lack of a proper evening meal and the cold bivouac out in the open have taken it out of him. Yesterday he got a bad deal as last man up and he is paying for it today. The decision is a hard one to make, especially since one of us would have to go down with him. The weather is perfect and we reckon that only about 600 metres separate us from the summit – if we make good progress we could reach it by evening. But Winni knows how vulnerable we are climbing Alpine style and how dangerous retreat can be when the weather turns bad and your reserves of strength are dwindling. Michi decides to set off down with Winni. We split up. The other two start abseiling, we carry on climbing. It is a sad moment for all of us. We had worked together on the mountain, we had set off

for the summit together and now, for them, the expedition was over.

It is slow going on the one-kilometre-long, almost horizontal ridge leading to the summit massif. Hour after hour passes as we climb up and down over and over again, with sections of grade VI climbing thrown in. With every metre it is becoming clearer that the summit is no longer within our grasp today. We had not allowed for so much time in our calculations. Even if everything went without a hitch, the safety reserves of gas and food would no longer be sufficient.

Towards midday, Jan and I broach the subject of turning back for the first time. Jan has had a bad feeling about it since morning. It is not that he has a specific reason for it. Apart from a cloud bank far away on the horizon, over in Tibet, the weather is optimal. Our progress, hampered by the terrain, is slow, for sure, but it is constant and the summit seems to be getting closer and closer, almost within reach.

We climb on. Hans and I take over the lead. A rock tower, which we had been hoping to be able to by-pass, turns out to be more complicated than we thought. Three pitches of mixed ground devour a further two precious hours. I reach the top of the last rock pillar, which breaks off abruptly, gently overhanging the summit structure 30 metres below. While Hans and Jan second the pitch I set up the abseil and then hand the lead over to them. They abseil into the notch and Jochen comes up to join me. As he attempts to haul in the rope that he has just jumared up it gets stuck. He climbs back down the 20 metres, cursing, in order to free the rope. Time for me to kick back and enjoy the view again. The afternoon sun is pleasantly warm and I start to doze off.

Jochen rails against his fate; the rope has got caught again and again he has to descend ten metres. "Jochen is tired", I think, "he has had no sleep for three days." Jochen . . . Now for the first time I realize just how slow all of us have become. Although we have been making steady progress, to be honest the last three days' climbing and the nights have robbed us of our reserves, those reserves of strength necessary to shift into a higher gear when conditions get more difficult.

I discuss the possibility of retreat with Hans and Jan. In bad weather this overhanging abseil from the top of the pillar would become an insurmountable obstacle unless we left a rope in place. But this would then mean we would only be

A lethal high-altitude storm rages out of Tibet, whipping across the ridges and high peaks of the Latok range

On the ridge between Latok II and Ogre II during the retreat. At this point things are still calm – there are clouds but hardly any wind

Hans Hocke on the retreat

able to set up one abseil at a time with the remaining three ropes on the descent from the summit – four of us at a time on a single belay? On the other hand, not to sacrifice a rope on the pillar would mean that, in the event of the weather taking a turn for the worse, we would have to descend the West Face Couloir, a gigantic avalanche funnel and a dangerous trap.

I look over towards Tibet. The bank of cloud seems not to have moved and looks to be far away on the horizon. But my mood has changed. I can find no tangible reason for it, but it has changed nonetheless. Only a few minutes ago I had been enjoying the peace and quiet during my rest on the top of the pillar. Now my stomach is churning, gnawed at by an inner restlessness.

I look at Jochen. He will soon be with me. I look down at Hans and Jan. They cannot see beyond the ridge, all they can see is the blue sky above them. I look across to the West, where, 200 kilometres away Nanga Parbat is etched against a sky of the deepest blue. I look at Jochen once more and ask him how he is feeling. He explains that he is tired, that he is no longer able to lead but that if we want to carry on he would go along with it. The conversation I had with Jan at midday goes round and round in my head again. He has been plagued by this bad feeling all day – not a tangible feeling, but neither is it a feeling he can suppress.

I look deep within myself.

I see us standing in the notch in a storm. Above us, the last tower on the ridge with its overhanging wall. We do not have the gear, we are too tired, we can no longer get up it. The hurricane rages across from Tibet and lashes the notch, robbing us of all our strength and dumping huge quantities of snow in the West Face Couloir, down which we now have to descend and the avalanches are now thundering. The notch offers no protection; on this terrain there is nowhere suitable to dig a snow hole. We have no tent, so we have to keep going, abseiling into the couloir. As we

lose height the force of the avalanches grows more intense. We are getting weaker and weaker, as darkness fall around us . . .

An unfounded vision? Am I getting hysterical? No, I am thinking rationally, weighing the chances and risks realistically against each other. I perceive the danger as real. And I make my decision. I shout across to Hans and Jan that we ought to turn back. They look back at me in disbelief. Only moments before they had left us without the slightest indication of a change in mood. And now they were meant to come back, climb back up the awkward abseil pitch?

I fix the rope and they jumar back up the rope to us. Retreat is now a fact, yet we nevertheless discuss my change of opinion as a team and, to my relief, the others arrive at the same conclusion: the difficulties and the sheer size of this mountain do not allow any further risks to be taken.

The sun is going down again as we reach our last camp. A further bivouac out in the open awaits us. During the night we are wrapped in clouds. No wind, just a light fall of snow. We take it as a warning sign and continue our descent well before sunrise. Light snowfall and wind alternates with sunshine; the weather is not bad but uncertain. Now that we have given up we are interested in only one thing – getting out of here! Not a minute longer than is necessary on this mountain. On the long, horizontal but knife-edged ridge between Ogre II and Latok II a strong wind blows up, sweeping our summit clear of cloud. We reach Advance Base towards evening and watch the spectacle of kilometre-long plumes of wind-blown snow streaming from all the ridges. A lethal high storm is raging on the high peaks of the Latok range.

Three weeks later we return to civilisation. In Skardu we learn of the tragedy that occurred on the day of our retreat only 30 kilometres away on K2. Seven climbers died in the storm – among them the Englishwoman, Alison Hargreaves, who since her success on Everest had achieved worldwide fame. They were literally swept from the mountain.

OGRE THUMB

Directly above Latok Base Camp at the edge of the Uzun Brakk Glacier is the Ogre Thumb, a freestanding 800-metre obelisk and one of the most beautifully formed granite towers in the world. For weeks the view of the Ogre Thumb had been part of the breakfast ritual as we poked our heads out of the tent each morning. Now that the Latok II chapter had been concluded the view alone could no longer satisfy our hunger.

The South West Face, the route taken by the German Alpine Club Training Expedition when the Ogre Thumb was first climbed in 1988, was declared as our next objective. 26 pitches of grade VI and VII, with three techno pitches for good measure. Hans and I intended to do the route, previously only climbed in expedition style, in a single day.

In order to realize this objective we would again have to climb as light as possible. We reduced our equipment to the absolute basics, taking only what was absolutely necessary and even dispensing with the Gore-Tex clothing. Only the second was to climb with a rucksack, and as small a one as possible. We wanted to average three pitches an hour, which would allow us sufficient time to abseil back down again in the daylight after reaching the top.

For the first ten pitches everything goes perfectly. It is a shame that a 15-metre bolt ladder proves impossible to free climb. My dream of a free ascent of the Ogre Thumb has to be prematurely buried – I finally manage it in 1997 by climbing a variation pitch. Nevertheless it is pure pleasure to be climbing at more than 5000 metres on best quality, warm granite.

It does not last long. Suddenly the clouds build and soon after the first snow falls. This time we do not give up; despite the imminent break in the weather we battle on upwards. After 18 pitches we stash the rucksack in order to make faster progress. We spur each other on into a wild gallop for the top. We reach it shortly before darkness falls.

After only one minute's rest we have to start down the abseils. Time is pressing. Twilight is already upon us and the headtorches are eight pitches below us in the rucksack. We have to get back to them while it is still daylight, otherwise we will have a ' no gear' bivi to look forward to. Hopefully the ropes will not get stuck! It is dark as I slide down the last pitch to the rucksacks but I have

At this altitude it is not uncommon to find ice in the chimneys. Hans Hocke at 5400 metres

Alexander after the first third of the South West Face of the Ogre Thumb

already memorized the terrain at the depot and can orientate myself sufficiently well even in zero visibility.

Eventually we get our torches back, the keys with which to escape an imminent bivouac. Meanwhile, the wall is now choked with snow and we are getting hypothermic in only our thin fleece jackets. We have to get down as fast as possible. By the beam of our headtorches we abseil down pitch after pitch in worsening weather, constantly aware that we must not confuse the ropes with the shadows they cast on the rock and accidentally slide off the end of the ab ropes. But everything runs smoothly and at eleven o'clock we arrive at Base Camp, exhausted and happy.

The Ogre Thumb, 5500 m. The route takes a line to the left of the boundary between light and shade

SPALDANG

The following morning I had not even managed to have a proper lie-in after the Ogre Thumb when the next temptation came knocking. It was Volker, the leader of a small Munich expedition that was using the same Base Camp, offering me the chance to join him on the first ascent of Spaldang. I was actually totally k.o. from yesterday but a first ascent! And so, the next day, as my own expedition team members set off with the porters back to civilisation, I joined Volker, Ruta and Spitz on the first ascent of Spaldang.

On the first day we climb the fixed ropes they had left on the lower section of the thousand-metre East Buttress. From the end of the fixed ropes we follow the firm snow ridge of the middle part and bivouac at its end, out in the open at an altitude of about 5000 metres.

The next morning. It is simply unbelievable! After a fantastic clear night the higher peaks of the Latok range are again shrouded in clouds and the weather looks anything but good. I am slowly getting the feeling that I am always in the wrong place at the wrong time. However, if you never try you will always lose! Ruta does not believe there is a real chance for the summit today and prefers to stay behind at the bivi site.

At eleven o'clock Volker, Spitz and I reach the Headwall, the crux of the East Buttress. One hundred metres high, overhanging, compact granite split right down the middle by a never-ending hand crack – the Salathé of the Karakorum.

Spaldang, 5590 m. The East Buttress is the central pillar, one thousand metres high, 35 pitches and difficulties to grade IX-

I had been able to make this crack out through the telescope. Full of self-confidence after my experiences in Yosemite, I set off up the first few metres. The hand crack runs upwards at an almost consistent width and will accept only a few of the pieces in our meagre collection of protection, which means I have to use them sparingly. In the thin air, every upward metre robs me of my strength and more and more often I find myself hanging from tired arms gasping for oxygen. It is only the practised routine of crack climbing that enables me to keep on recovering and to get my depleted reserves of oxygen back to normal.

Climbing the Headwall means we have now breached the last rock belt barring the way to the summit ice field and the final steep upsweep. Like some wild animal, I circle around looking for the easiest way up the five-metre high monolith of the summit block. But is is Volker, not me, who has the honour of *Ius primi ascensus* and I wait my turn, even though it is hard to do so. Heart racing, Volker does the boulder problem at 5590 metres and is the first person to stand on the summit of Spaldang. Four days later, in perfect weather, Ruta, who had had to listen to our radio call announcing our success and was unable to do a thing, also stands with Volker on the highest point.

Alexander climbing the almost perfect, one-hundred-metre-long hand crack on the Headwall

Ruta Flohrschütz on the snow ridge of the middle part of the East Buttress, just before our bivouac site

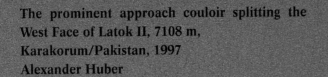

The prominent approach couloir splitting the West Face of Latok II, 7108 m, Karakorum/Pakistan, 1997

Alexander Huber

The West Face of Latok II, so impossible in 1995, still held me in its grasp. The thousand-metre Wall of vertical granite held such an attraction for me that I was simply unable to let it go. Barely two years later I was back again and this time Thomas was along on the trip as well.

We are sitting in a four-bed room in the Paradise Inn in Rawalpindi, a hotel with a largely euphemistic name. Thomas, Toni, Jan and I are the vanguard of the '1997 Latok and Ogre Expedition'. At the start of every self-organized expedition to Pakistan there are days of organizational work to do in Rawalpindi, which lies only a few kilometres from the new capital Islamabad, a city created out of the bare earth after the founding of the State of Pakistan in 1947. This work is unavoidable and to a certain extent irritating. Insurance has to be taken out for the porters and the liaison officer; a deposit of 5000 US dollars made in the event of a

THE WALL

BIG WALL CLIMBING ON LATOK II

Two-way traffic on the Karakorum Highway

helicopter rescue; we shop for basic provisions; register with the police, without which nothing happens at all; and we still need a bus to take us into the Karakorum... It is stupid to have the whole team waiting in Rawalpindi while all this is taken care of; firstly, it is expensive and secondly those who are just waiting around are unnecessarily subjected to the risk of infection. This is why there are just four of us on the trip, three from the Latok team and Jan, the leader of the two-man Ogre Expedition.

The 'briefing' is what they call the ultimate audience at the Ministry for Tourism, at which it is revealed whether or not everything has been correctly organized and all the various duties have been fulfilled. During the briefing itself it is not really possible to rectify mistakes. In 1995 I watched with horror as the entire Spanish Uli Biaho Expedition was sent home simply because their liaison officer was dissatisfied with his equipment.

This morning the rest of our team should be arriving at the airport. We hope to get the briefing over by midday since the bus to Skardu, the main town of the province of Baltistan, goes in the afternoon. We would normally have gone to pick the lads up at the airport at 6 o' clock but shortly before 5 there is Jochen standing in our room. The news is bad, very bad. Everyone apart from him has managed to miss the plane in Munich. For a moment I think I am in the wrong film. I can't believe it; I am speechless.

Before I can really start thinking clearly again the others appear. At first I think it must all have been just a bad joke but the story that Jochen tells us is too crazy to have been made up. On the flight to London he had spent some time thinking about what the reduced Latok team of Thomas, Toni and I could do instead – maybe an attempt on the Ogre with him and Jan? Then the solution turned up: the rest of them arrived in London three hours late but still in time to catch the plane. All apart from Schlesi. Jochen explains that Schlesi had vanished without a trace shortly before they were all due to drive to the airport together. In the resultant chaos all of them missed the plane, with the exception of Jochen, who had travelled to the airport independently of the others. Subsequently it was down to the persuasive, rather than the medical, skills of our expedition doctor Bernd to convince another airline to take the late arrivals to London at no extra cost. The problem was not solved yet, however; they were still missing Schlesi.

Crisis meeting in the hotel room. Reinforcements have now arrived in the shape of Conrad, who has flown in on his own from America. We sit on the beds under the rattling ceiling fan that swirls the stuffy city air around the room. On the information sheet from the government it clearly

Ismail and Kassim

states that all the participants have to be present at the briefing – all of them.

I know that the Pakistani officials do not always take the written word too literally, their decisions tend to be made more on the basis of gut feeling, but unfortunately the Minister is in a bad mood today. Although the participants' details have been

available for scrutiny for a while now, Conrad's are missing. Stay calm, Alex – even if you are boiling inside and any minute you could go crazy and strangle the living crap out of him. I watch the ceiling fan out of the corner of my eye as it tries to

BUT UNFORTUNATELY THE MINISTER IS IN A BAD MOOD TODAY

cool the stressed-out head of the Minister with some nice fresh air but succeeds only in blowing some loose bits of paper from the files onto the floor. I show the Minister his letter of reply, in which he had confirmed the personal details of the participants now present. Visibly unimpressed, he answers only that we will still have to wait until Conrad's details have been vetted by the Secret Service. Under no circumstances may we leave the capital today; and the bus is waiting! Finally, the Minister graciously agrees to allow the rest of the group to leave. However, as leader of the expedition, I am obliged to wait with Conrad until the Secret Service gives the all-clear. We should then get ourselves an additional trekking permit for the journey to Skardu and, so we do not stray from the authorized path, we are assigned a guide. Carefully, I broach the subject of Schlesi but the Minister chokes off my approach with an

Shortly after leaving Skardu, which we finally reached by bus, we travel through the desert-like dune landscape in the mighty Indus Valley

imperious wave of his hand, "No possible." The next day Conrad and I do manage to acquire permission to follow the others from the Minister, who is clearly in a considerably better mood, but on the subject of Schlesi the high-ranking representative of the Pakistani people remains obdurate.

Finally we are out of that hole, out of the heat and the city smog. For reasons of economy we travel with our guide on the public bus. It is very cheap, very crowded, very interesting and a very intensive olefactory experience. We literally rub shoulders with the Pakistanis and after 24 hours the special smell of our fellow travellers is as familiar to us as our own.

During the night things get even more exciting.

I feel like I am watching a Western with John Wayne and Clint Eastwood as the two men wordlessly square up to each other, revolvers in hand, ready for the shoot-out. But nothing happens and after a minute or so they scream at each other again for a bit, put their weapons away and turn.

I am too much of a Middle European not to breathe a huge sign of relief as the journey continues. The starter motor is tortured, the gear-box raped, the driver takes the rest of his anger out on the gas pedal and with a black cloud of smoke we are off again, the bus just a little the worse for wear. Tough country, tough customs . . .

We have been driving for a while high above the Indus Gorge as day breaks. After the oppressive

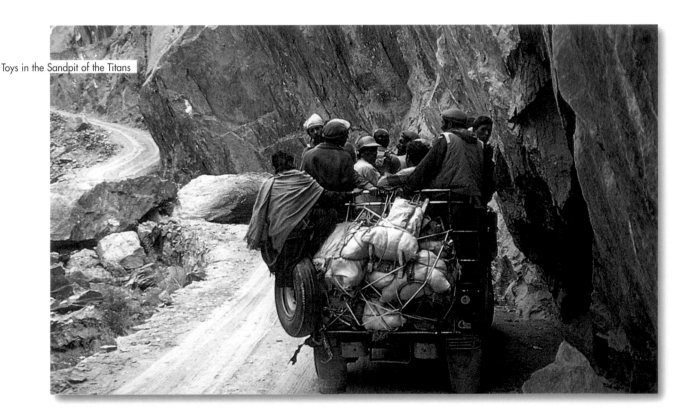

Toys in the Sandpit of the Titans

After our over-tired driver has demolished the rear end of another bus it all develops into hand-to-hand combat. Things get heated as 50 Pakistanis square up to each other, shouting and hitting one another in an attempt to apportion blame in a situation where it is glaringly obvious whose fault it is. Although the bus is insured through the company, for the driver it is not a case of sorting out who is responsible for the damage but a matter of personal honour, which he is obliged to defend. After a quarter of an hour the potentially violent mob splits apart and our guide pulls me by the shirt back onto the bus with the words "Gun, gun!"

damp heat of Rawalpindi it is now dry and hot here in the highland desert. The first of the Himalayan ranges collects so much moisture that behind the mountains there is hardly any rain all year long. It is difficult to imagine that somewhere around here there is snow falling and glaciers and mountains standing about.

The climate inside the bus is still like a sauna. Sixty people produce a whole lot of sweat and since the windows do not open the relative humidity is approaching 100 per cent. I look back with longing on the nice, cold nights bivouacking on the North Face of the Eiger in winter. Was that really only

orters in the high mountain desert of the Karakorum

three months ago? Far below on the banks of the Indus burned-out buses tell of the last acts of other drivers who have fallen asleep and bear mute witness to the Pakistani's attitude to life. "Inshallah" – if it is God's will we will arrive in one piece – in a bus full of passengers in the hands of a driver who constantly falls asleep. We head for Skardu at top speed, powerless to do anything about it.

Camp, about sixty deutschmarks; he is hoping for at least 2000. Haggling is the name of the game here; after all, we are in the Orient. After half an hour we are deadlocked – I stick at 1600, he holds out for 1800 – but Ismail understands that he will not be able to negotiate more for the porters. We are not a Japanese expedition that pays over the odds and thus spoils the wage structure, as has so often happened in recent years, with the result that we have to do battle with the profiteers and the

"INSHALLAH" – IF IT IS GOD'S WILL WE WILL ARRIVE SAFELY

Ismail and Kassim are waiting for me at the Hotel K2 in Skardu, just as they were two years ago on my first Latok expedition. Ismail is actually the cook but he organizes everything else as well. With his help, the kerosene and the rest of the foodstuffs have already been acquired. We can set off tomorrow.

As usual when an expedition comes to town there is a crowd of Baltis milling around the hotel fence. They come looking for work as porters. I negotiate a price with Ismail for him, for Kassim and for the porters. I haggle with him over every last rupee. I suggest 1200 rupees for the four days to Base

local porters have to compete with people from other valleys for whom the high porter wages mean it is worthwhile abandoning their normal work at home.

With a grin, Ismail finally agrees to 1600 for the porters but not without thinking about himself too, "Okay, okay. Money for porter no much, but enough. Porter no need so much. But rupees for Ismail no good!"

The Jeeps for tomorrow's onward leg of the journey arrive in the evening. Instead of the six Jeeps we ordered there are seven in all. The explanation we are given is that six would not have

The real Karakorum Highway: the Biafo Glacier

Balti porter

been enough for us. Again we haggle, this time about every piece of luggage on the Jeeps. "Too much, no possible. Road very bad." Comments like this regularly wind me up. You can come here whenever you want and the "road" will always be "very bad". Only the massive threat of changing to a competitor at this late hour, and only after we start unloading the Jeeps again, does the owner of the Jeeps give way. Suddenly they are all fully loaded and the seventh Jeep departs.

The next day we are away before sunrise. We have to make an early start since the rough track that leads for 100 kilometres through the Braldu Gorge crosses several glacier streams and these swell hugely in the afternoons, rendering them impassable.

The Braldu Gorge leads right into the central region of the Karakorum. When talk turns to the Karakorum you think of huge mountains surrounded by equally huge glaciers and a unique icy landscape. But whatever images the sound of the word might suggest, the meaning is actually rather sobering, for in the Turkic language Karakorum means nothing more than 'black scree'. It is a more than appropriate description of the Braldu Gorge. Like toy cars, our Jeeps drive through this sandpit of the Titans. The route along the deep defile of the raging Braldu does not afford

us a view of the icy giants of the Karakorum and the dry scree slopes are only seldom interrupted by the lush green of fields irrigated by the glacial streams.

Our motorized journey ends at Askole. Lying at a height of 3000 metres, this is the last continuously inhabited village before the high mountain desert. Hundreds of Baltis are waiting here for us, waiting for work as porters. Occasional work as a porter has become a regular part of the lives of the inhabitants of furthest Baltistan. Although it earns them the equivalent of only 12 deutschmarks a day and they will certainly never grow rich on it, load-carrying is the only possible way for them to get any money at all. The work is much sought-after and the crowd of job seekers correspondingly large. To create order from the ensuing chaos is the job of the Sirdar, the leader of the porters. He differs from the rest of the Baltis only inasmuch as he can read and write a little and can speak a few words of English. These skills alone are sufficient for him automatically to assume a lead role in the society here. It is down to the Sirdar to distribute our eighty 25-kilogram loads among the porters and to ensure that throughout the walk-in to Base Camp none of the loads go missing with any of the porters.

At Askole we finally leave civilisation behind as we head off with our 80 porters into the remote high mountains. To begin with our route climbs higher and higher along the old hunting paths of the Baltis, beside the raging torrent of the Braldu fed by the gigantic glaciers of the Biafo and Baltoro regions, and we soon see the first six-thousanders – rough, glaciated granite needles, the true landmarks of the Karakorum.

A little col away from the main path to the Baltoro Glacier, firm ground beneath our feet for the last time, and then it's onto the 60 kilometre long Biafo Glacier. At first, this does not look like a glacier at all; tons of scree and boulders cover the ice masses. This stretch is hard for the porters; up and down, up and down they carry their loads between granite blocks weighing many tons, come wind

The West Face of Latok II

come weather, through the rain, snow and the glaring heat of the sun. A single blanket provides their only protection from the cold nights; they use this to pad their loads too. Then there is the little bag for their chapattis; a handful of flour mixed with two handfuls of water and baked on a stone over an open fire, washed down with tea flavoured with salt and yak butter, undrinkable for us Westerners. Life up here is hard; everything reduced to a minimum, yet I can still sense their quality of life. The Baltis are happy with simplicity – laughing, joyful people.

Reinhard Karl wrote some sobering thoughts on the Baltis and their way of life but he was on his way back from a failed attempt on K2 then, deeply frustrated, and maybe particularly sensitive to

The last day for the porters. Taking a rest in front of the granite towers of the Latok Range

anything negative. I see it differently; when I look into the faces of the Baltis I cannot fool myself. They are content with their life, more content than many in our civilization, and they have a job to do that gives them both a bit of variety and a bit of cash.

After three days and 30 kilometres on the Biafo we reach Baintha, one of the classic Balti camps on the edge of the Glacier. Baintha lies at about 4000 metres and it is here that we leave the ice of the Biafo and follow the Uzun Brakk Glacier into the heart of the Latok group. The tension is almost tangible. The Baltis are excited because tomorrow they can drop their loads and return to their villages but above all because tomorrow is pay day and they will have earned about a third of their yearly income. We are excited because apart from me all the others know our objective only from photographs and tomorrow for the first time Latok II will be standing there right in front of us.

We have established Base Camp at 4400 metres, at the confluence of the Uzun Brakk Glacier and the nameless glacier that comes down from the foot of the Rakhiot mountainside, in a spot dubbed 'Fairy Tale Meadows' by the German expeditions of the 1930s – the name is understandable, for after leaving the dry rocky desert of the Indus Valley you arrive at a vegetated area just like the most beautiful alpine meadows. Like on Nanga Parbat over there, our Base Camp is also on a fairy tale meadow; hemmed in by gigantic glaciers, protected by their lateral moraines is a spread of lush green fields through the middle of which a small stream winds its way to feed a small, shallow lake in which we can even bathe when the weather is fine. After our porters have deposited all the loads in the middle of the meadow and I have paid them all off we are all at once alone, surrounded by the savage rock towers of the Latok group. No wind, no avalanches, no stone fall – in a way, the silence is somehow unsuitable for this awe-inspiring rocky landscape.

First off, I head for the moraine with the telescope for a good, long look. Was my planning correct? In August 1995 the huge rock fall caused by advanced exfoliation had put paid to any chance of climbing the West Face of Latok II. That was

why this time I had set the start date for the expedition for six weeks earlier, hoping to find better ice conditions. I breathe a deep sign of relief – the calculation seems to have worked! The couloir to the West Face is deep in snow and

Alexander at the 'Balcony Camp'. The couloir rises in a monotonous sweep to the foot of the Big Wall

Base Camp at 'Fairy Tale Meadows'

Toni Gutsch and Alexander at their Portaledge Camp

snow-white, with no sign of the telltale black streaks that indicate stone fall. By increasing the magnification I can study the rock structure of the upper thousand metres of the West Face. The sunlight cast shadows and causes the cracks and groove systems to stand out sharply against the smooth, featureless sweeps of vertical rock. Each of us looks through the telescope and attempts to arrange the pieces of the puzzle, joining together identifiable features to form the ideal line.

Before we take our first steps onto the mountain we organize the equipment for the big wall. One thousand metres of vertical wall take time to climb. We intend to spend 20 days in this granite labyrinth. That means reducing the provisions to a bare minimum. Every gram is weighed and accounted for. Per man and day we take 125 grams of gas, 300 grams of freeze-dried food and 200 grams of carbohydrate bars. For 20 days and four men that means 40 kilograms of food and 10 kilograms of gas, in addition to which there is all the bivouac and climbing gear. The whole lot has to be carried up the couloir to the start of the Wall at 6000 metres!

14th June. After the second night at Base Camp I wake up with heavily swollen eyes and a blocked-up nose. It has got me; here of all places I get a bad cold. For four years I have been working towards this wall, I have spent a hundred sleepless nights tossing and turning in bed because the image I have of the Wall will not leave me in peace. And now my body refuses to co-operate. I am uncertain now. Can I shake off the infection? Will I manage to deal with the altitude?

Bernd, our expedition doctor, has got it even worse than me. He has been plagued by a cold for several days now and slowly but surely the infection seems to have brought him to his knees. After another bad night he decides to go down to Baintha for two or three days. It is only 400 metres lower but that is generally enough to put the brakes on a little dose of altitude sickness. Since I am no use either with my sniffles I decide to go down too and keep Bernd company. Meanwhile, the other three transport the gear, establish

Advance Base Camp at the foot of the Wall and day by day start getting themselves used to the increase in altitude.

Unfortunately, Bernd's first night at lower altitude has not had the desired effect; the problems he is having with the upper respiratory infection have instead grown worse. Bernd and I are just talking about the options still open to us when a familiar voice draws near. Schlesi arrives, accompanied by six porters. He has somehow managed to convince the government in Islamabad to allow him to travel on and catch up the expedition without any further documentation.

Due to his weakened state of health Bernd decides to go lower with one of the porters. Should there be any considerable improvement he will come back up to join us. If not, he will set off early on the return journey to Europe. He leaves us two big boxes of medical supplies but without his specialized knowledge they are largely useless to us. We will be spending six weeks in the wilderness without medical attention and can only hope that nothing happens.

The next morning I go back up to Base Camp with Schlesi. The others have made good progress, Advance Base Camp has been established and the first loads have already been shifted up into the couloir.

24th June. Thomas, Conrad and Toni have reached a height of 5600 metres in the couloir and established the 'Balcony Camp' there. The start of our Big Wall is getting closer and closer but with every metre gained my hopes of being along for the ride are growing fainter and fainter. It starts to snow now – a change in the weather. Within a short time the whole mountain is in motion. Everywhere there is spindrift pouring from the walls and snow sliding down the couloir. Those three up there need to get out of there fast. Every minute counts now as the fear of being swept away by an avalanche forces them back down the couloir. They race down, jumping over the new snow slides as adrenaline drives them on. After an hour they reach safe ground, just before the first big avalanches roar down the couloir.

Over the next few days more than a metre of new snow falls at Base Camp, where we are now all assembled. This is my big chance. If my body can beat this infection during the period of bad weather then I hope to be able to make up for lost time and get acclimatized.

After Bernd's departure we are hit by a further setback; Michael contracts a kidney infection and also has to set off for home. He leaves the camp, crestfallen, accompanied by Ismail.

During the bad weather we often discuss the tactics we will employ to make further progress. How many can we have climbing the Wall at the same time? How best to approach the huge wall? Franz and Schlesi decide on their own line; they are fascinated by a groove system that splits the face 200 metres to the right of the point at which we had planned to start. That leaves Thomas, Conrad and I for the original route.

On 2nd July the weather improves. The very next day I go up to Advance Base Camp at 4900 metres with the others, right up to the foot of the West Face. Tomorrow is the day; the couloir awaits.

At 1:00 AM early bird Conrad tears us from our dreams, then from our sleeping bags. Because of the stone fall we want to play safe and use the coldest hours to get to Balcony Camp before sunrise. I take my first steps in the couloir today. No one talks much; each of us is experiencing the same oppressive tension before the most dangerous part of our project, this ice chute in which everything from above collects.

We traverse horizontally beneath an 800-metre high rock wall into that unimaginably huge funnel,

It doesn't get much more featureless than this: El Capitan granite in the Karakorum. Toni on the 11th pitch (A3/VI+)

The last few metres of climbing at the end of a hard day's work

trying not to think about the rock avalanches of 1995 when I experienced a whole night of heavy bombing. This time things are quieter but not necessarily any less dangerous. For 30 minutes we climb up beneath an overhanging sérac before we are able to traverse right onto seemingly safer territory. Conrad's eyes have changed; the usual quick-fire humour has gone. He looks up, then shouts something, the meaning of which I fail to understand completely at first but which later becomes clear; a phrase that describes the situation in the couloir perfectly, "Dancing in the ballroom of death with the fat lady of faith." From now on we refer to the sérac affectionately as 'The Fat Lady'.

It is hard going but it does at least take your mind off the danger lurking above and focuses your thoughts more on what is happening inside your own body. You just have to hang in there, motivating yourself anew, metre by metre, to get the 30 kilos on your back higher up the mountain. At 8 o' clock we arrive at the more or less safe Balcony Camp, perched beneath a rock overhang on the right hand edge of the couloir. We dig out another little platform and pitch a second tent in the lee of the overhang. Worn out, we sit outside our tents, nothing more than four little dots in the couloir, that gigantic waste disposal pipe for avalanches. Above our heads the Big Wall stretches up into the blue skies. The dimensions are overwhelming and are magnified by the homogeneity and monotony of the ice field but still it fascinates us, it dominates us, it determines our every move.

The next day, while Toni and Conrad ferry another load of provisions from ABC to Balcony Camp, Thomas and I fix the 55 degree ice slope to a height of 6000 metres, up to the start of the thousand-metre-plus Big Wall. Again we hack a platform out of the ice to serve as a camp for the first pitches up the granite wall that now soars up directly in front of us. Still poorly acclimatized, we spend the night back at Balcony Camp.

We set off again in the middle of the night. Even though we know that this is the safest time of day there is still an all-pervading sense of tension. Below us the beams of the headtorches are lost in the yawning abyss; somewhere up above is another hanging sérac, a fickle foe lurking unseen in the dark above us. The force that pulls us upwards is our motivation finally to start climbing that wall. Up in the camp Thomas and Conrad decide to go down again and spend two days

carrying up more provisions to stock the camp, while Toni and I will start climbing today. Fifty carabiners, 20 Friends, 30 nuts, 15 pegs, six different Skyhooks, hammer, aiders, fifi hooks – a well-dressed Christmas tree standing in the snow below a kilometre of granite. It was only three days ago that I left Base Camp, only halfway healthy,

Conrad Anker on the 14th pitch (A3)

and now here I am standing in the thin air at 6100 metres above sea level about to start on the biggest challenge of my life so far. My acclimatization deficit made itself felt for the first time today. As we climbed the remaining 100 metres from the camp to the start of the route I had to give my load to Toni on more than one occasion. With the best will in the world I was unable to pump the necessary oxygen into my lungs.

As I set off climbing my brain cells have already been suffering from oxygen deprivation for several

so we abseil off and organize our bivouac at the foot of the wall. The first night at 6000 metres. Again and again we wake up gasping for air. Our respiratory systems have not yet adjusted to this

A FICKLE FOE LURKING UNSEEN
IN THE DARK ABOVE US

hours. Legs shaking, I step up onto the first foot holds – I really have got the wobbles now! A slab at about grade VII, badly protected, quite run out in places. Right in the middle of things I often do not know exactly what I am doing right now or where I am exactly. My field of vision shrinks to just the next hold and it is only routine that gets me up in a reasonably solid fashion.

Finally I reach the lower end of the crack system I had been aiming for. Relaxed now, I clip the first

Thomas at 6800 metres on the West Face – the summit is getting closer

good piece of protection. Oh God, my head! I am nearing a state of complete intoxication. With hammer and pegs I work my way laboriously over the first roof. Luckily aid climbing is not as strenuous as free climbing and I quickly recover. After the second pitch it slowly starts getting dark

altitude and react with Cheyne-Stokes breathing – two minutes with no breath followed by panic-stricken gasping for oxygen. Nevertheless, the next morning Toni makes a phenomenal lead over a damned smooth-looking roof on rurps, knifeblades and a hook move – the first A3 pitch is per-fect! Thomas and Conrad take over from Toni and I for the next two days, pushing the route to 6450 metres before a bad weather front on 9th July sees us all reunited back at Base Camp.

13th July. Yesterday brought bad weather again. Toni and I are back on the Wall. From the end of the fixed ropes we left during our retreat I climb a perfectly formed layback flake until it runs out into totally holdless rock. With skyhooks biting on tiny edges only a few millimetres wide I traverse rightwards. Calmly, I search for the right skyhook for the next mini-edge when – damned hook! – I find myself hanging head down ten metres below. Right then, start all over again. Back up to the top of the flake and traverse right again. This time I use the hammer to improve the edge; the hook bends under the load, but it holds.

The following pitch is pretty spicy stuff too. After a delicate slab, climbed exclusively on skyhooks, comes a moderately difficult hairline crack about ten metres long. The next bit, a six-metre flake, is just sitting there waiting to explode. The only thing holding it on is the ice at its base; it seems to be floating there, completely detached, above our heads. I do not fancy a flying lesson with this little baby in my arms and creep off to the side on hooks. After this pitch my nerves have had it; time to swap leads.

As Toni and I abseil back down at sunset after two more pitches we meet up with Thomas and Conrad as arranged. They have been hard at it the whole day long and have managed the backbreaking job of dragging up to 6500 metres all the gear they need for eight days living on the vertical Wall. While these two will spend the next two days pushing the route, the same torture is what awaits Toni and I. At least the Wall is so steep and compact that we do not have any problems heaving up the haulbags. Nevertheless it is late

Behind us the Ogre, ahead of us one last snow slope, beyond that – nothing

afternoon by the time our camp is finally ready and hanging next to the others'.

We are using the Portaledges for camps. Imagine them as being like folded-out prison bunks stuck to the Wall like swallows' nests. For us, the Wall is to become a bit like a prison. By day we perform our forced labour by climbing; in the evening the cold of the night forces us back into our little cells, in which everything is accomplished within one square metre of space instead of the entire house we would otherwise have at our disposal, from drying clothes, tidying up and sorting out the gear for the next day to melting water, cooking, eating, sleeping. . .

Shortly before sunset Conrad and Thomas slide down the ropes after their day's work to hot soup and the evening meal already simmering on the stove. We all eat together, nice and cosy. There is not a breath of wind, it is totally calm and the last rays of the sun make for a pleasant temperature, bathing the Wall in a glowing red light, one last blaze of light and warmth before darkness and cold gain the upper hand.

It is one of those moments when I know why it is that I always return to the mountains. I enjoy the peace and quiet, happy that I am one of the privileged few able to experience this unique natural spectacle. Down in the valley it has been dark for a while now, while right back on the horizon Nanga Parbat still shines brightly. I think of Hermann Buhl; it must have been at exactly this time that he stood on the summit, in the evening as the sun was sinking. . .

The morning is less romantic and peaceful. During the night the temperature fell to minus 20 degrees and we are sitting on a West Face where the sun will not reach us until early afternoon. While the neighbouring Ogre, the main peak of the Latok group, basks in morning sunlight we sit in the cold and try to get out of the starting blocks as quickly as possible. But breakfast, attending to urgent business, getting dressed, getting back up to the previous day's high point, climbing – it all happens at a reduced speed with numb fingers. We long for the afternoon hours, when the sun literally floods the Wall and the temperature rises to around the zero degree mark, allowing us to climb without gloves and dream on the stances of Bavarian beer gardens with *brezen* and *weißwurst* if there is nothing urgent to attend to.

17th July. We have reached a height of 6800 metres. Up here the Wall appears less steep and

After a thousand metres of vertical
granite, we reach the snow dome of
the summit – the contrast could not be more extreme

Conrad on the summit of Latok II

featureless. It looks as if it might be possible to reach to summit from here in a day but if we were to mount an attempt tomorrow we would be in danger of over-stretching our reserves. We are completely exhausted from the hard labour of the last few days; our extended stay at an altitude of more than 6500 metres has taken its toll. We deliberate and discuss the situation. The stable weather over the last six days gives us confidence; there is not even the slightest sign of clouds in the sky. There is no reason why the weather should suddenly take a turn for the worse the day after tomorrow. We decide to take a rest day.

At midnight on 19th July we set off. This is to be our day, the day when, for me, a four-year-old dream is to be fulfilled. It will be so nice when the work is done and I can put away the tools, when I can stand back and admire my work as something I myself have created and which for this very reason is so dear to my heart.

Four small lights work their way upwards through the night. At 4:00am, just before sunrise, we reach the top of the vertical Wall and an altitude of 6800 metres. No, for God's sake no! Please not now, not today, not here. It cannot be true. 200 kilometres away, over on Nanga Parbat, a huge storm front has formed, filling the whole width of the horizon. A gigantic firework display, every second a glaring blue flash somewhere on the horizon. Back in 1995, at 6600 metres on the

◆ I ENJOY THE PEACE AND QUIET

North West Ridge, the weather had forced me to turn back and now, two years later, am I to have the same old shit but at 6800 metres? Don't say we have thrown away our chance of summiting by taking that rest day?

It will be a race against time. In just one hour it might all be over, driven back down by a snow storm. The last lap to the summit is a terrorist attack on our nerves. The mixed ground is harder than we expected; I can only make extremely slow progress on this tricky section. Up ahead of me the rock leans back in the light of my headtorch.

I stand on the front points of my crampons on a slab covered by a wafer-thin veneer of water ice. Two metres above is the ice of the couloir that would lead us to the summit. Carefully, I place my axes in the lower, hollow layer of ice. I am not happy with it.

I think about it (amazingly enough I can still do this up here). We are not in the Alps here or on any other little frozen cascade; we are at almost 7000 metres in the Karakorum, at the very end of the world, and if you fall off here . . . Your only life insurance is you yourself, so climb back down, climb slowly, go down step by step, there is no sense in doing anything else, this is not ice that is

Toni, Alexander and Thomas on the summit of Latok II, with the Ogre in the background

the easy-angled ice of the summit couloir. I shudder when I look down. Dynamic moves on ice at 7000 metres! At first sight too risky but I could not have solved the problem safely with conventional ice climbing techniques. It was only by stretching up quickly enough that I could avoid weighting the hollow lip of ice.

Luckily it does not continue in the same vein. It

Toni abseiling down the West Face. 200 kilos of gear had to be carried back down the mountain

100% guaranteed to hold your weight, go on, slowly, step by step. . . .

I take two fast steps – not downwards but upwards. I watch myself as I tear out the axes and sink them dynamically into the solid ice above, just before my body topples over backwards out of balance. I am now standing on

grows light, the climbing becomes increasingly easy, we make faster progress but, more importantly, the storm front has stayed where it was back on the horizon and above us there is steel-blue sky. Toni climbs what looks to be the last steep section. In front of us lies a snow slope, beyond that – nothing.

PROTECTION

Bird beak

Nuts

Skyhook

Angle

Friend

A thousand-metre new route requires a lot of equipment to protect the climbing. This, in addition to the provisions, is responsible for the enormous weight of our haulbag.

We wander up the last few metres to the highest point together. We have done it, as a team. All four of us together on the summit. The summit is just a small, flat pile of snow at a height of 7108 metres but it is more, much more than that. For us the summit means the end of a desire that had captivated us for years. Now we are free – even if it is only for a short while.

The descent proves to be an adventure in itself. We lower the haulbags down the couloir, the state of which has deteriorated rapidly in recent days due to the warmer weather. A huge rock avalanche tears two of our haulbags away down into the abyss. A hundred kilos of gear, half of the equipment we had with us on the Wall, is gone. During the night at 5600 metres a fist-sized rock rips through the tent and the foot section of my sleeping bag. Now we are no longer really

safe from stone fall even under the rock overhang. The mountain shows us in no uncertain terms that we should no longer be here.

We clear and strip the whole Camp. In order to carry the large quantity of equipment back down we have to climb down the couloir twice during the night. And during this night, although we are so close to safety we can almost touch it, for the first time we are really afraid, afraid of what might happen.

At 9 o' clock we finally set foot on the glacier, on safe ground. Just two hours of tiresome descent back to Base Camp, where Ismail and Kassim will welcome us with a huge celebratory feast. Luxury at 4400 metres.

Only now, in complete safety, do we feel we have really done it. For sure, the summit was the high point of our undertaking but the real objective, to return safely, has only now been achieved.

 FOR US THE SUMMIT MEANS THE END OF A DESIRE THAT HAD CAPTIVATED US FOR YEARS

LATOK II

Reinhold Messner

The first ascent of the West Face of Latok II in the Karakorum was only achieved at the second attempt. In making the climb Alexander Huber, who was on both the first attempt and the successful summit bid, showed that he was capable of learning from mistakes, according to the 'attempt – error – new attempt' principle, and demonstrated that the Big Wall method can be transferred to the seven-thousander region.

The summit wall is more than a thousand metres high, for the most part vertical and very compact in structure. Twenty years ago walls as steep as this would only have been attempted at three thousand metres lower, ten years ago at a thousand metres lower and in ten years time the most difficult walls of the eight-thousanders will be climbed directly.

What is it that the Big Wall on Latok II, which the Huber brothers and their partners managed to climb, this new dimension? Without doubt it is the combination of the high level of difficulty and the high altitude. The high standard of climbing required after a dangerous approach in a remote corner of the Karakorum led the summit team into the kind of 'limit situation' which has been typical of classic mountaineering for two hundred years. Only the most extreme levels of difficulty, exposure and responsibility – judged by contemporary standards – can be the ingredients from which pioneering achievements are made.

> It has always been the innovators, who forge ahead into the new dimensions – greater levels of difficulty, higher mountains, less technology – and go down in mountaineering history as the most successful climbers of their era, not the record breakers, who use existing structures to go faster, more often and higher. The 'best', apart from the competition climbers, have never existed and the most successful were respected for their lifetime's achievements – Angelo Dibona, Riccardo Cassin, Walter Bonatti, Chris Bonington. There were always a couple of pioneering achievements that stood out in the foreground, which at the time could not be repeated. The best age for this seems to be thirty. Thus the Huber brothers have all the prerequisites in order to gain membership of that tiny circle of those who push ahead into that distant world, where our game is much more than just a sport. « R.M.

The danger is part and parcel of such dimensions of mountaineering and the skill lies in avoiding it, step by step, day by day, for months on end.

The fact that such peak performances find less public recognition than a record-breaking race in the tracks of hundreds of amateur mountaineers up the pre-prepared Tourist Route on Mount Everest is merely due to the notional prestige attached to the highest mountain in the world. For experts, this mountain has lost more and more of this prestige but for the public at large it continues to be so significant because of its size.

It is not the eight-thousander-collector climbing in the slipstream of the trekking tourists and mimicking the successful sportsman who gets the vote for the 'Best Mountaineer of The Age' but the one who treads new paths, treads these paths for himself and finds his way back to civilisation from the vertical chaos in the Death Zone, ready for the next attempt – and the next challenge.

CHO OYU

THE FIRST EIGHT-THOUSANDER

The Tichy Route slants up from the right across the sunlit flank of the mountain: Cho Oyu, 8201m, Himalayas/Tibet, 1998
Alexander Huber

The Big Mountain. Reinhard Karl called it a building without a staircase, a building without storeys, a building without doors, a building that becomes a prison when you try to get to the top of it. For him, it was the ambition to stand right up there on the top that represented the invisible prison bars. And freedom? Freedom would only be his again after the summit.

Mountaineering means climbing mountains, high mountains too. "What is a guy like you going on Cho Oyu for?" was the astonished, uncomprehending question people asked me. Me, the rock jock, stamping around in the snow on Cho Oyu? Trudging along, gasping for breath, wrapped up like a Polar explorer. What business did I have scrambling around the flat icescape of the Turquoise Goddess? After March 1998, as more and more of my acquaintances learned of my plans, I was confronted with this question increasingly often and always gave the same banal answer: "What am I going to do there? Go climbing!"

The plan to climb Cho Oyu was, in principle, nothing more than a logical development in my

the toughest and best mountaineers. Yet, for me, they always remained a goal; I never stopped dreaming the dream, even if I had in the meantime neglected the mountaineering theatre in favour of sport climbing.

The object of my desires, Cho Oyu, is generally regarded by the experts as an 'easy' eight-thousander. However, this is merely because

There is not a single road in the entire Solu Khumbu region. The transport of equipment and provisions still takes place predominantly on the backs of the Sherpas

Stone inscribed with the words 'Om mani padme hum' ('Oh you jewel in the lotus blossom')

mountaineering ambitions. Climbing, for me, in all its various forms is simply the realization of a fixed idea and after climbing my first four-thousand-metre peak in the Alps the high mountains of the Himalayas also became part of my childhood dreams, became just such a fixed idea.

In the last few years, of course, the 8000-metre peaks have lost much of their air of inaccessibility; they have become the playground of the masses and, to borrow a phrase from Tom Wolfe, a 'bonfire of the vanities'. The nimbus has become dulled; they are no longer the sole preserve of

climbing Cho Oyu by one of its least demanding routes is said to be 'easier' than the so-called 'hard' eight-thousanders like K2, a fact that is often overlooked. At 8201 metres, Cho Oyu is still the sixth highest mountain in the World and this alone gives an indication of its difficulty, difficulty that has very little to do with mountaineering ability. Technically, it requires little more from the climber than one of the more demanding 4000-metre peaks in the Alps and any accomplished alpinist possesses the necessary technical skills to tackle it. Even a height of 8000 metres and more demands no specific qualifications; practically any healthy person has the ability to acclimatize and adapt to these high altitudes. What really defines the difficulty here is the risk to which anyone who contemplates climbing at such altitudes is exposing himself. The body is pushed to the very limits of endurance, where it becomes dangerously susceptible to malfunction.

Thus, the great art of climbing the highest mountains on earth is not just a matter of reaching the summit. What is crucial is the way in which you reach it; namely, with a clear head and sufficient in reserve. Being in full possession of your faculties is the only way to master unforeseen problem situations and to be in a position to compensate for any weaknesses and return safely from the Death Zone.

Such considerations were instrumental in our decision to go for Cho Oyu rather than one of the more difficult 8000-metre peaks. My previous experience at altitude was limited to 7100 metres in the Karakorum and 6700 in South America with Barbara. Eight thousand metres in the Himalayas – a good thousand metres more – represents a completely new dimension. We both had every reason to view our objective with the necessary respect.

We took the preparations every bit as seriously as the objective itself. We acquired the best available equipment, since Barbara and I could not allow ourselves even the slightest sign of frostbite – for sport climbers no mountain in the world is worth climbing if it is going to mean amputations. Fingers and toes as collateral for a Faustean pact with the Devil? Not with me you don't! I want to be off climbing in sunny Yosemite after Cho Oyu . . .

The right physical build-up is also important, of course. It wasn't that we were planning to make a record-breaking ascent of Cho Oyu but a solid ability to perform guarantees fast climbing at altitude, shortens the time spent in the Death Zone and allows the body to produce enough warmth to combat the danger of frostbite.

However, the most important part of the preparations was the acclimatization phase, we felt. Two weeks before the start of the expedition Barbara and I set off to acclimatize by trekking through the Everest region. The highest peak we

Prayer flags at almost 5000 metres in the Gokyo Valley. Signs of the religious belief of the Buddhist Sherpas are present everywhere in the Khumbu

climbed was Gokyo Ri, an easily accessible peak of almost 5500 metres from which we were to enjoy breathtaking views of the mountains. Four of the six highest mountains in the world could be seen in close-up: Mount Everest, Lhotse, Makalu and – Cho Oyu. Our objective was so close we could almost reach out and touch it; only a few kilometres and a height gain of 2500 metres separated us from the summit. Nevertheless, we still had a long way to go, since even from here the easiest route to the top of Cho Oyu was still via Katmandu and the high country of Tibet.

The first big hindrance started developing while we were still trekking. I managed to contract an inflammation of the tonsils that was so painful that there was nothing else for it but to take antibiotics. You think you are fit and healthy then suddenly your body refuses to co-operate. Back in Katmandu, and before we continue on to Tibet, we have a few free days breathing space, a good opportunity to take in some of the country and, for me, to take it easy and get myself well again. Most of the time I lay in bed enjoying the warm, damp air of Katmandu and in time the symptoms did disappear. The inflammation had subsided but I was still unable to shake the illness completely for the duration of the expedition. A week later, as we set off from Katmandu heading for Tibet the inflammation started up again. There was no other option but to stay behind at a lower altitude for the time being, while Barbara walked on ahead to Base Camp with the others and our gear.

Doubts arise; they gnaw, they bite, they eat away at you, they drag you down into the depths of depression, into a slough of despond that only you can pull yourself out of again. Does staying behind mean the premature end to all your dreams? Will

On the way to Gompa Tengboche, which is the religious centre of the Sherpa people in Tibet

there be enough time left to reach the summit before the monsoon makes climbing impossible? Tingri, in the middle of a plain in the high country of Tibet. This waiting for an improvement in my health becomes a kind of psychological martyrdom. Time slips by. Damned pains in my throat. There is a huge mountain up there but what is making my life difficult are ridiculously tiny bacteria. Ultimately, however, waiting turns out to be a wise decision as, slowly, my body gets the inflammation under control. Still weak at the knees I stumble off, then impetus gains the upper hand and after three days' walking I arrive at Base Camp at 5800 metres.

From now on everything moves really quickly. The very next day I go up to 6300 metres with Barbara to establish the first camp. After a rest day at Base Camp we go back up to Camp 1 again and spend our first night there. Sleeping at this altitude exacts its price; in the morning we do not exactly feel well so take a rest day up there. The next day we feel significantly better and climb with full loads to

The rural exodus shows no signs of abating; thousands still flock to the poverty of the Katmandu slums

7000 metres and our camp for the summit push. We leave the loads there and descend to Base Camp.

That should be enough preparation for the summit. We both feel good and are only waiting for good weather, as are Horst Fankhauser, the custodian of the Franz Senn Hut in the Stubai Alps, and Georg Simair, a mountain guide from St. Ulrich near Lofer. The weather has been unsettled for two weeks now, with almost daily high storms – the Fate of the 8000-metre peak. We do nothing at Base Camp for two days and then the weather

Storm in the high country near Tingri

Although still one hundred kilometres distant, the peaks of Mount Everest, Gyachung Kang and Cho Oyu can be clearly seen in the clear, dry air of the high Tibetan plateau

situation improves. Is this the window? We hope so. In the morning we are still undecided but finally the four of us set off and climb up to Camp 1. During the night Barbara and I are plagued by headaches – and again the nagging doubts surface. Are we really sufficiently well acclimatized?

Breakfast time. Both the headaches and the bad feeling disappear. The most important things, caution and impetus, return. Onwards, ever onwards. And again the rucksack weighs heavy as we climb the snow ridge and a 70 degree ice

◆ BUT FIRST I HAVE TO GET UP THERE

bulge to reach Camp 2.

The afternoon up there at 7000 metres could have been relaxing but it is so hot that we lie almost naked in the tent when melting snow for a brew. We sweat as if in a steam bath – what a crazy world!

To redress the balance the night is bitterly cold. I toss and turn in my sleeping bag and down jacket, too nervous to sleep. My first 8000-metre summit is close enough to touch, even though there is still a height gain of 1200 metres to come. You dream without sleeping, thinking about what might happen; you are seized by the idea of going right to the top today. An eight-thousander is an eight-thousander, it is one of those objectives you set yourself as a mountaineer and one to which you submit yourself completely. You are not interested in the fact that it is 'only' the 'Normal Route', or that it is 'only' an 'easy' 8000-metre peak. You have to get up there, do it for yourself and then you have to get back down again too. Then you have something that no one can ever take away from you, an experience that you have fashioned yourself in your own little world. Cho Oyu – perhaps it will be the springboard to the really big ones, the really wild things . . . who knows?

But first I have to get up there. Even dwarves start small, according to the film maker Werner Herzog, but this is not really a fitting comparison, for Cho Oyu is big, damned big, and there are still 1200 metres in vertical height to go, which up there is half an eternity. I cannot sleep, I am too nervous and that is something I cannot do anything to change.

The air from our breathing has condensed on the inner walls of the tent to form a layer of frost; every tiny movement of the tent causes snowfall. We have to get busy, so we melt snow; during the day breathing is so strenuous that we will need plenty of liquid. During the day – that is still so far away that I still can not really imagine it.

But then it is 2 o'clock and the countdown begins. We get ourselves ready, slowly, no hectic activity. At three o'clock Horst and Georg set off. All at once panic breaks out in our tent, panic that we are too late, that we will not be able to catch up with them. Totally superfluous, but that is the way it is. We are not ready yet but we do want to stay close to the other two. It takes Barbara and I a full half hour to get all our clothing on and crawl out of the tent, out into the Himalayan night.

The other two already have a pretty good head start. Breaking trail through the snow looks to be laborious but not too exasperating. So I walk, stamp, struggle on, step by step. After two hours

Barbara Hirschbichler above the sérac at 6800 metres

◆ IT IS A MOVING SPECTACLE, AWE-INSPIRING

I catch up with Horst and Georg. Closing the gap so quickly has cost me valuable strength but I still want to make my contribution to the job of breaking trail. Now things get tough; I can only break trail for a short time before digging in behind them again, gasping for breath, but confident. At 7500 metres we take our first rest. We have not done the first half yet but we need a break to get rid of the tunnel vision caused by the hard graft and watch the grandiose spectacle of the sun rising. It is a moving spectacle, awe-inspiring.

Just as Horst and Georg are setting off again Barbara joins us and I wait with her. Tongues

sticking to the roof of our mouths, we attempt to choke down a muesli bar. Half an hour after the others we set off from the rest place too.

We are getting slower. We started too fast and overdid it climbing the first 500 metres in two and a half hours. But the weather could not be better, it is not even 7 o'clock in the morning yet and we have Horst and Georg up ahead going strongly. No need to panic and no reason as yet to turn back! We work our way slowly upwards, one foot in front of the other, our breaks becoming more frequent. At some stage, much later, shortly before 12, I see Horst and Georg. Soon now we will all stand together up there on the summit where the climbing finishes.

This time, however, there is no joy on reaching the summit. I can feel my infection starting again. I am wide awake. All my senses have suddenly become highly sensitized. I can feel that the situation is threatening – at high altitude respiratory infections are the fastest way to contract pulmonary oedema or an inflammation of the lungs. I still do not feel in any way hampered by the infection, I still feel strong and I am still thinking clearly, but now I cannot afford to waste any time, I have to get myself out of this oxygen-deprived Death Zone, every minute spent here could worsen my situation. I only have one thought: get down, now, as fast as possible. So, no euphoria, no feeling of happiness, no pride, no time to look and enjoy.

While Georg waits for Barbara I immediately start down with Horst. Driven by an inner restlessness I descend at high speed, losing height metre by metre and only two hours later Horst and I are back at Camp 2 at 7000 metres. An hour later Barbara arrives with Georg.

Cho Oyu during the approach march to Base Camp. The clouds above the summit tell of a storm at high altitude

Horst climbs the 70° sérac at an altitude of 6600 metres. The technical crux of the route, it now has less sting through the placement of fixed ropes

On reaching the camp we have returned to civilization. A lot of people have come up to this camp today and will make their summit bids tomorrow. A few of them walk over to congratulate us and a Sherpa gives us some tea. Although we are still at 7000 metres we feel great, almost as if we were back at Base Camp. The

6 o'clock in the morning on summit day. We are still climbing in the shadow of the North West Flank but behind us Menlungste and Gaurishankar are already lit by the sun

tension of the last few hours evaporates, the load is lifted, there is no more pressure on us, just kick back and relax, free at last . . .

The questions come thick and fast:

"What was the snow like?"

"Pretty firm but it's still hard going."

"How long does it take from the top edge of the plateau to the summit?"

"It goes on for ever. An hour and a half for sure."

"What was it like up on the top?"

"No idea. I was only there for maybe a minute. I was shitting myself about this infection I've got. Didn't want to do anything else other than get down, just get back down."

So there was no summit joy. Up on the summit, the fear of the potentially serious consequences of my infection had been electrifying and had made me do the only right thing at that moment – get down the mountain and out of the Death Zone as fast as possible.

Now I am happy to be back at the camp safe and well. It is a moment of genuine happiness, something I had not experienced much of during the course of the expedition. Even though – or perhaps because – Cho Oyu was my first eight-thousander, there were only a few brief moments of enjoyment. There was a lot more tension than fun. And yet, an 8000-metre peak is and remains an exceptional experience. The extremely high level of

95

Above the clouds: Horst and Alexander on the last few metres to the summit

But the appeal of the eight-thousanders really does lie solely in the search for adventure. The simple fact that there are no peaks of 9000 metres and higher and that our human ambition always directs our attention to the fastest, the best and the highest means that they cast their spell over us. People are always trying to get higher. Here on the eight-thousanders they can get higher than anywhere else.

Back home in my cramped office I relive my Cho Oyu climb. I read about it and constantly leaf through the books of Reinhard Karl. "Eight-thousander mountaineering is a game with high stakes", he writes, " you have to try and not give up, over and over again. Whether you are successful is decided by Fate, or Allah or God. The joy that comes from standing on the top of an eight-thousander is not something that happens quickly. The road to the 8000-metre peaks is a slow road to happiness, the happiness of one who has suffered, rooted deep within you, forever unforgettable."

I carry on reading and flicking through *Berge auf Kodachrome*, Reinhard Karl's last book. It ends with some photos of Cho Oyu. The last picture is of the memorial pyramid for Reinhard

commitment and self-will required to climb it gives you that feeling – even if nowadays climbing the eight-thousanders by their Normal Routes have only few surprises in store and offer only limited adventure, since nothing is really unknown any longer. The only unknown quantity is you yourself as you push forward into the icy heights for the first time. The fact that many others are climbing the same route means the mountain is robbed of its savageness; the hurdles become smaller. Sophisticated logistics and the comfort of inclusion in a large group reduce the adventure to your own personal level of experience and to a large extent the rest of the adventure can be calculated.

Georg approaching the Yellow Band at 7500 metres. Although never really difficult, the climbing requires constant concentration

Adventure, the spice of life of the mountaineer, is something I find only when I go to the places no one else goes to; when I am at the mercy of the sheer size and danger of the mountain; when, lost on a huge mountain face, I look for ways out; when I feel tested to the limit.

Karl in the Gokyo Valley, with a slab of rock engraved with his name and below, Cho Oyu and the date he died – 19-5-82. Sixteen years later to the day I stood on the summit of the mountain that was to have been his next big peak, the one he never climbed and that became his grave.

CHO OYU ALTITUDE TEST

Reinhold Messner

There is no eight-thousander more suited as a test of one's own ability at high altitude than Cho Oyu in the Everest region. During the main season in spring and autumn the mountain usually has several dozen groups camping and climbing on it and the route is then well prepared. You can find route markers all over the place, high camps every few hundred metres and fixed ropes on the steeper passages. Danger, exposure and hassle are reduced to a minimum.

In spite of the tracks and the convoys of porters, the low oxygen pressure and the risks of a sudden snow storm, with white-out conditions and low temperatures, remain the same as they have always been – life threatening. Nowadays of course, a mountaineer on the tourist route to the top of Cho Oyu need not spend so much time up there as Herbert Tichy did during the first ascent in 1954 and the danger of suffering frost bitten hands or feet has been reduced to a minimum with the special clothing now available.

A flying visit to the Death Zone is enough to discover that not only one's own strength diminishes with the increasing altitude, but also one's general ability to assess things accurately. Brain and muscles are deprived of adequate oxygen supplies and it was this experience that Alexander Huber wanted. Maybe he will take the second, third or fourth step and take his skill and his readiness for action onto the eight-thousander walls.

High-altitude mountaineering *en masse* as a hunt for prestigious summits, with organizations, animation and local leadership, can be countered by nothing other that the ascent for which you yourself are accountable, in a small team, with a minimum of equipment and a maximum level of difficulty. The longer the convoy of consumer mountaineers becomes, the more exposed the goals of the pioneers must be. Should the one group meet the other on the summit, they can still climb down together.

EL NIÑO

NEW DIMENSIONS IN FREE CLIMBING

**Alexander in the Black Dihedral, 5.12c,
El Capitan, Yosemite/California, 1998
Thomas Huber**

American Dream, easy living, highways, the
fat growl of an eight-cylinder, customized truck,
fastfood on every street corner. Westcoast Rock on
the radio, fingers beating the rhythm on the
steering wheel, sun shining. Well, here we are!
Back in the land of the superlative again.
Everything is bigger, higher, fatter than back
home in good old Europe. Our destination in
this, the seems-it-never-rains State of California,
is, as usual, the Flowerpower Metropolis of San
Francisco, the only city in the world the locals
refer to simply as 'the City'. Flying from Europe to
the West Coast of the USA you gain yourself a
whole day, so we are using it for a quick stopover
at Conrad Anker's place on the drive to the
Yosemite Valley.

We are cruising East along Highway 120 in our hire car. The sun setting over the Pacific bathes the gnarly old oak trees strewn among the golden yellow prairie grass in a delicate shade of pink. Even the light is something special in this land of plenty; it shines with the unnatural light of a Hollywood film set, like looking at the world through a coloured lens filter. The situation inside the car, on the other hand, is rather less romantic,

in his lectures from now on. We, on the other hand, are off on an adventure that, for us, represents a new dimension and a new level of quality. Conrad wishes us well and his parting words fire us all up for the trip, "You'll pull that thing off. Just do it. Yeah!"

We have already far exceeded the 35 m.p.h. speed limit. Just a few more miles now and we'll be on a different time-scale, too. Life in Yosemite Valley is

◆ "YOU'LL PULL THAT THING OFF. JUST DO IT. YEAH!"

with four of us, plus 300 kilogrammes of luggage crammed in there. Alexander sits with the haulbags on the back seat, with Heinz, Peter, three rucksacks and me up front, all squashed together in this too-small car, the only thing over here that is not larger than life.

We drive the overladen eight-cylinder the 130 miles to Groveland, about 30 miles from Yosemite National Park. Perched on a hill a little way out of town is the Old Priest Ranch, the home of Conrad. Alexander is happy finally to be freed from his prison as we all clamber out and stretch our legs. Conrad does not appear particularly surprised to see us standing at his front door; he knows all about our plans and has been expecting us.

In customary 'American style' we stand on the terrace of Conrad's ranch, slurping the fine black coffee – Pete's Coffee – and catching up with the latest climbing gossip – who's been doing what, when, how and with whom. When we try to prise a bit of info on North America Wall out of him, he puts on the typical grin of a Californian sonny-boy, a look we remember well enough from our Latok expedition. "Hey boys, I got something for ya – too hard for me but just right for you guys!" Conrad pulls his 'secret topo' of a possible free route up the right side of El Cap out of his Big Wall pouch. We study it in surprise; it is almost an exact copy of our own prospective line, the Free Right Side.

Only last week Conrad had been up on the North America Wall with two friends checking on a possible free line; the result is a sketch with a lot of question marks, but it gives us a foretaste of what to expect when we get to the Valley. Jetlag prevents us sleeping, and we chat late into the night about the Free Right Side – after all, that's why we are here.

Our first morning in California. Conrad is already rushing about again, jetting from one slide lecture to the next for The North Face; his El Cap time is over for this year, he will only be talking about it

something very special; the 'Yosemite way of life' is life in a microcosm in the wide-open land of America. It was the first climbers in the Valley that shaped this lifestyle, a style that has persisted to this day. The fundamental characteristics of this sub-culture could not be simpler:

1. *Climbing is the most important thing in the world.*
2. *Money is of secondary importance to the modus operandi.*
3. *The Laws of Nature apply. Public Enemy Number One are the rangers.*
4. *The higher the level of craziness the better and freer the lifestyle. The motto: Be lazy, be crazy, just be a climber!*

Fascinated by the feeling of the place, hundreds of climbers from all parts of the world come to the Valley year after year to live out this philosophy; some come once and stay forever. We are exposed to it all for just a limited amount of time. For a whole seven weeks we are freaks, acrobats on a thousand-metre precipice, an additional attraction for the tourists at no additional cost. The climbers, the long-haired freaks who hang around in the dust at Camp IV and drag their huge haulbags up the walls of El Capitan or spend hours on end working on the same boulder problem, are as much a part of the tourists' sightseeing programme as the famous waterfalls, where they attempt to recreate for themselves Ansel Adams' rural idyll.

Just occasionally, one of the tourists will even manage to summon up the courage to ask one of these wild heroes why they should voluntarily choose to court danger and spend days on end living in a vertical desert of rock. The answer, when it comes, is usually brief: "It's fun to be crazy!", whereupon the tourists generally react with an incomprehending shake of the head. For them, the greatest adventure imaginable consists of the Valley Floor Tour, crammed like sardines into one of the Green Dragons, the 20-metre-long

Looking for a free
climbing solution

open-top tourist shuttle buses...a completely different dimension.

We turn off into the one-way traffic system in the Valley. Our first port of call is El Cap Meadows, the prayer mat of many a climber; from here that they can pay homage to the Great Captain of the Sport of Climbing. At the same time, the Meadows is a 24-hour live cinema with the biggest cinema

"What a piece of rock!" – at the start of the North American Wall

also wanted to be one of the pioneers of modern free climbing and to this end had selected the Magic Line on El Cap, the route up the thousand-metre South Buttress, the Nose. The idea was as presumptuous as it was brilliant. It had only one failing; and that failing was Ray Jardine himself.

No one believed his contention that it was possible to free climb this route, even at some stage in the far distant future. The Valley climbers were generally of the opinion that the central section of El Capitan was only climbable by artificial means. That, however, was not the approach that Ray Jardine advocated. The standards he worked to had nothing to do with the Nose and the problems it presented; all that mattered to him was his own climbing ability, and that alone should determine the difficulty of the route.

For Jardine, the Nose was merely a climbing frame on which there were no insurmountable barriers. His aim was to create a route at the upper 5.12 level of difficulty on the one-kilometre-high buttress. The plan was known only to him and to a few initiates who were to help him realize it. After the Stove Leg Cracks, a virtually holdless section of face climbing, prevented him from making any further progress. Jardine chiselled the solution to this problem into the bare rock – and with this act of vandalism Jardine created his own

◆ IT IS TOTALLY AUDACIOUS, BRILLIANT IN CONCEPT, BUT WILL INVOLVE A LOT OF DAMNED HARD WORK

screen in the world. We are positively knocked out by the view of El Cap from the Meadows – "What a piece of rock!" On this monolithic colossus of granite, climbing history was written, ground-breaking victories celebrated and painful defeats suffered. This wall was the focus for many a heated discussion about the fundamental ethical principles of climbing and the object for territorial claims for 'new land', as a result of which many a protagonist made a belly-flop into the dust of the venerable Camp IV. But primarily, El Cap was always the stuff of which dreams and visions are made; it was, and remains, the breeding ground for new and great challenges.

Ray Jardine was the first to attempt to transfer the ideas and principles of free climbing to the El Cap canvas. He numbered among the most high-performing climbers in America and with his invention of the 'Friend' introduced an important technical innovation to the sport of climbing. He

sporting gravestone. The Valley climbers, who had followed Jardine's machinations on the Nose with keen interest and were not in agreement with his ethical views, advised him to cease his preparation of the Nose immediately. Jardine stood alone with his vision, he had no one on his side and thus no chance of pushing through his idea. So he buried his dream of turning the Nose into a route he himself was capable of free climbing.

This relic from an ethical cul-de-sac was, nevertheless, the act that prepared the way for a free ascent. Without the Jardine Traverse the original, classic line of the Nose would still not have been freed, even today. Lynn Hill used it in 1994 and her first redpoint ascent in just 23 hours hit the male-dominated scene of El Cap aspirants like a whiplash crack. With Lynn Hill's tremendous achievement the old sins of the past were forgotten. The Jardine Traverse is now an integral part of American climbing history; to

The North American Wall is named after a huge black diorite deposit that bears a striking resemblance to the shape of the North American continent

continue to get annoyed about past deeds is surely the wrong way. It is better to learn from the past, to view critically possibly misguided developments and to fight to ensure they do not reccur. What is crucial is what is happening now, in the present.

My brother followed suit in 1995 when he made the first redpoint ascent of the Salathé Route to the left of the Nose. His photographs of the Headwall were seen around the world and the result was that free climbing on El Cap received a new impulse and experienced a real boom. More was possible than had been thought possible just a few years before. Even the North America Wall, a route which had indeed been attempted free, again became the focus of considerable interest, particularly for the Americans, who certainly had no desire to see the Free Right Side also snatched from them by Europeans!

Lynn Hill made several serious attempts on the classic North America Wall, but the tremendous difficulties and atrocious protection on the lower third of the Wall forced her to give up. Protecting these pitches with expansion bolts would have contravened the rules of the 'Yosemite school of climbing', where placing bolts is only allowed on first ascents or as yet unclimbed variations. So the climbers racked their brains and searched for alternative ways to crack the problem of the lower part of the wall. Debate raged and soon the first rumour surfaced that Lynn had in fact free climbed the North America Wall, all apart from a few metres, but this turned out to be nothing more than a rumour.

Bullwinkle, a photographer from the Valley who knew that we were going to be pitching our tents in Camp IV at the beginning of September, attempted to fire Lynn Hill up for a futher attempt on the route with a phone call in mid-August – it would have been a good photo-story for Bullwinkle. When she told him she would be there at the beginning of October he told her he thought that she would probably be too late for the North America Wall.

A dense network of over 80 routes and variations criss-crosses the thousand-metre-high South East Face, the 'Right Side', of El Cap, almost all of them extremely hard techno-routes. The first route on the face was done in 1964 by the legendary Royal Robbins, with Chuck Pratt, Tom Frost and Yvon Chouinard, in nine days of hard labour. The North America Wall, named after the huge black diorite deposit whose outline bears a remarkable similarity to the North American continent, was for a long time rated as the hardest Big Wall in the

Climbing on tiny edges and chickenheads – Thomas on
a blank section of the Black Dike, 5.13b/X–

5.8
"The Northpole"
5.10a
5.9

"Eismeer"
5.12c

5.12b
"The Dolphin"
5.10b
5.12c
3
5.11a
5.12d
"The Slalom"
5.11a
5.13b
"Black Cave"
"Rotten Island"
5.12c
"Black Dihedral"
5.12c
"Endurance Corner"
5.12a
Manpowered
5.9   Rappel
5.13c
"The Royal Arch"
5.13a
5.6
5.10c
5.11c
3+
5.8
"Calaeras Ledges"
5.11d
5.11a
"Galapagos"
5.13c
"The Missing Link"
5.13a
"The Black Dike"
5.13b
5.9
5.5

world and was a milestone that defined the era. Alongside this route a new milestone of our own era could now be set, for it was here that we reckoned on finding the best climbable rock features for our free ascent on an otherwise repulsive and featureless wall of rock.

Alexander screws the telescope to the tripod and we compare our sketches with the magnified image we get. At the end of our studies we are no

touch El Cap again. I lean back against the rock and tilt my head back at an angle, my face pressed against the warm granite . . . It's good to be back. All my dreams and desires converge upon a single point, and this point lies one thousand metres above me. In between there is nothing but a vertical desert of yellow granite. Our aim is to cross this desert on foot, on all fours in fact, without any kind of artificial aids, but right now it

The free route up the endless sweep of granite follows the huge veins of black diorite. Alexander on the Galapagos pitch, 5.13c/X–

wiser but our preconceived ideas on the Free Right Side project have been confirmed. It is totally audacious, brillliant in concept, but will involve a lot of damned hard work. Neither Conrad's 'secret topo' with our own scribbled additions nor the coldly analytical view through the telescope can provide us with a clear answer to the decisive question: does a free climbing connection exist between the first and last holds on the proposed route? We do not know the answer, yet that is exactly what makes it so exciting.

We waste no time, we have collected all the necessary information and can profit from the attempts made to free climb the line over the last few years. We intend to use the original start as a last resort only, since we know that Lynn Hill did not have the best experience of her life on the first few pitches. At a feature known as the Footstool, a prominent rock formation at the start of the New Jersey Turnpike, 50 metres to the right of the original start of the North America Wall, two alternatives present themselves, either of which might provide the combination required to crack the lower section of the face up to the Cavaleras Ledges.

We carry two rucksacks with sufficient water to the base of the Wall. It is always an exciting moment when, after a long absence, you get to

all seems so very far away, so unachievable. It is this unachievability that provides the impetus for us to dare to attempt this thing that we call adventure.

The first 50 metres are a gift. A groove system, well-endowed with good holds, lands us on the top of the pillar of the Footstool, a large stepped rock plateau. But the granite then becomes mercilessly compact and steepens abruptly. There are two realistic possibilities of reaching the crack and chimney system that begins 150 metres above: either up the classic New Jersey Turnpike, or via a left-right dogleg detour discovered, but not climbed, by Conrad and Kevin Thaw. The advantage of the New Jersey Turnpike link is that most of the old bolts and rivets have been replaced by solid new bolts. According to Conrad, the dogleg variation would go but it would require a lot of drilling and that would mean a considerable amount of extra effort.

With a compact battery-powered drill of the type common in Europe this would not be a problem, but these are forbidden in the Valley. Here, all the bolt holes have to be drilled by hand, using a hammer and hand-held drill bit, like in the early days. On the hard granite this means 30 minutes per hole and plenty of sweat, dirt and strength. For two climbers attempting to make a free ascent of

Muir Wall this all seemed like too much of a waste of time and energy. They took a drill up with them and were promptly arrested by a group of several rangers as they topped out. A day later they were sitting behind bars in the John Muir Jail for contravening Park regulations. For us, this was out of the question. We would rather voluntarily accept a brief spell of convict labour than actually become convicts ourselves.

Alexander jugs up the fixed ropes left by Conrad and Kevin and studies the rock structure on the New Jersey Turnpike. I kick back, take a break and

Alexander emerging from the Black Dihedral, 5.12c/IX-, heading for the climax of the route, the big roof of the Black Cave

listen to his running commentary and his final verdict on the first pitch – it will go, and will involve face climbing at around the 5.13 mark. The second pitch, he reckons, is crazy, out-there stuff: above him, the wall bows out steeply and looks like streuesel cake. Everywhere you look, ironstone deposits sprout from the granite to produce a superabundance of hand and footholds. These are the marvellous little rock formations we call 'chickenheads'. Alexander thinks the pitch will be a pure pleasure to climb and will certainly present no problems for us as we try to turn our

idea of the Free Right Side into reality. Beyond the Chickenhead Wall the face lies back a bit and the crack/chimney system, the key that unlocks the passage to the middle section of the wall, is so close you could almost reach out and grab it.

I can hardly believe what I am hearing. This would mean we have taken only one day to find the solution to a problem that had others tearing their hair out for years. Confident now that Alexander will shortly find the ideal line, I sit forward on the very edge of the rock pulpit.

From here, I have a wonderful view out over the Valley. It's always the same picture, seemingly unchanged by the years. The Merced River weaves its calm and relaxed way through El Cap Meadows. The sluggish, placid river down below has lost nothing of its ability for psychological torture – when you are up on the granite wall almost dying of thirst there is nothing you would rather do than leap into the flood, mouth open wide, and drink your fill of the sparkling water.

The only departure from this eternal, steady rhythm was caused by the Merced River itself when it burst its banks and flooded almost the entire Valley, taking houses and cars with it and destroying most of the campsites. Only Camp IV, the homeland of the climbing freaks, remained untouched – God looks after his chosen sons . . .

In accordance with American principles, everything was rebuilt within the shortest time span possible, while the business-minded Park authorities attempted to clear Camp IV, even though it was safe from flooding, to make way for hotels and more permanent accommodation. Up to the present, however, the protests made by both American and international climbers have been successful. It would be an outrage indeed if this historic campground, the hub of the climbers' universe, were to fall victim to the ravages of tourism.

For decades now, climbers from all the nations of the World have congregated here to experience 'the Yosemite way of life', the 'Separate Reality' of Camp IV culture. This internationalism brings a new impetus to the otherwise unchanging, rigid structure surrounding the permanent residents of the Camp, who sit there quietly rusting away. Exceptions exist, of course, among them Scotty Burk and Dean Potter, who earn their money on El Cap rescues and by cleaning windows but spend most of their time following their favourite pursuit – climbing. At the other end of the spectrum are long-standing veterans who hardly

The second pendulum traverse. Thomas
spends hours swinging back and forth,
looking for a solution

climb at all any more yet still have an incredible amount to say on the subject. They generally hang out at Sunnyside, where they doggedly demonstrate their support for a particular brand of beer.

A hundred metres above me, Alexander lets rip a heart-rending curse, rudely disturbing my Valley reveries. Just a few metres before the start of a prominent chimney, a slab a mere three metres high has called the whole project into question. It might go somehow, according to Alexander, but how exactly remains a mystery to him. He ties into a separate rope and goes looking for a better solution.

Meanwhile I pendulum across to the left on the fixed rope to check out Conrad's and Kevin's idea. It looks perfect. The Black Dike, a diorite vein starting from the same point of the Footstool, splits the orange-coloured and totally featureless sweep of granite. Conrad has already placed three

With Peter Jantschek on the summit plateau of El Capitan

crimp, saves a thousand-metre project from failure! This brings the dimensions into sharp focus once again. They are as diverse as nothing else, yet are mutually dependent – each matchstick crimp, each fingernail flake, each little unevenness in the rock contributes to reaching the last hold after a thousand long metres.

The Galapagos Pitch, which takes us back into the dihedral and crack system of the New Jersey Turnpike, is the hardest pitch yet. Our left-to-right dogleg has cost us a huge amount of work, but it was worth it – we now have the victor's medal for the first stage in our pocket. We plan on spending the next five days on the wall in order to check out and equip the middle section from Big Sur to the Black Cave. It is the most exciting part of our project and the one with the most question marks hanging over it, in particular the two pendulum traverses and the big jutting roof high above – the Black Cave.

The next three pitches up to Big Sur present no significant problems from a free climbing point of view. It is our haul bag that puts the brakes on. Towards evening, men and materials are all finally assembled at Big Sur, a ten-metre-long by one-

bolts on the Dike, which ends after 40 metres at a ledge. It looks well climbable, at least from the brief view you get of it from the pendulum it does. The 20-metre link into the Galapagos pitch of the Continental Drift is, with the exception of a few metres, strewn with chickenheads and Galapagos itself, which leads back right to the crack system of the New Jersey Turnpike, ought to be possible free, according to Conrad. I am certain that this is the best line. Alexander is happy too, since he has still not found a more amenable alternative. Richer for the experience we abseil back down and pay our first visit to one of the few positive new developments in the Valley, the Garden Terrace,

◆ AND SO A TINY DETAIL, A TWO-MILLIMETRE CRIMP SAVES A THOUSAND-METRE PROJECT FROM FAILURE!

with its 'all you can eat' budget deal. And here we have another new experience: with this type of restaurant you generally feel a lot better before than after, with a belly stretched to busting point.

Work starts the next day. We remove loose flakes, clean out dirt-choked cracks and work out the best and most amenable line through the black diorite streak. The most awkward part of our exploratory work is placing the necessary fixed protection. The 20-metre section between the Black Dike and Galapagos almost puts paid to the whole project. Directly above the stance on the link pitch, an awkward featureless section of the face blocks access to the enjoyable Chickenhead Pitch above. A loose granite flake, the only handhold, snaps off under our weight and temporarily buries all hope of linking the section. It seems at first as if we have again stumbled into a blind alley, but while cleaning the fresh rock scar with a toothbrush I discover a two-millimetre-wide crimp – just enough to make the moves climbable. And so a tiny detail, a two-millimetre

metre-wide ledge on the edge of the North American Continent, situated right on the dividing line between the golden-yellow granite and the black diorite. The outline looks astonishingly like the Pacific coastline; the golden-yellow granite stands for the sea, the black diorite for the mainland. We are still on dry land, but tomorrow we will cut loose and dive into the golden waters of the Pacific Ocean.

The world up here is a strange one. The shimmering haze on the hot golden granite really is like an ocean – a *fata morgana*, a wishful notion in this unbearable daytime heat. Everything is twisted through 180 degrees. After a certain time we too are pretty twisted; the longer we live in the vertical plane the crazier we get. Our thoughts and our actions are directed solely towards surviving in this unique biotope. The basis for this survival is our climbing partnership, a self-sufficient team responsible for and accountable only to itself. Tied into the climbing rope, this is a temporary long-term relationship, where everything has to function under the most cramped conditions

Thomas leads the Royal Arch, 5.13c/X–

accompanied by a characteristic El Cap soundtrack. During the day it is determined by the swallows, with their ceaseless, never-varying song, and the hawks swooping past us with breathtaking speed on their plummeting nose-dives. At night it is the shrieks and howls of the other temporary residents on the various routes of this biotope that make up the musical score, as they scream away the tension that has built up during the day's climbing. Singing in unison it is not, and it is certainly not characterized by mutual tolerance either. Yeeeaaah Yuuuuuhuuiii . . . Shut up, you asshole, I wanna sleep . . . Huuuuiiiiaaaaahhhh . . . Fucker shut up . . . Aiaiaiaiaaiiiiihhhhyyyaaaa . . .

It goes on like this for half an hour and we crawl into our portaledge. We are sleeping better and more comfortably up here than down in the Valley; there are no irritating little stones poking us in the back and the 500 metres of air below our bivi ledge is certainly conducive to sweet dreams. By morning we have recovered well from the hardships of the previous day's sack-hauling.

The first rays of sun light up the Black Cave. The black overhang gleams with such unreal golden colours that we almost do not recognize it. But this inviting view lasts only a short while; as the sun climbs higher in the sky the Black Cave darkens and soon reverts to its customary inhospitable and fearsome appearance. But we are not there . . . yet.

The next big obstacles are the two pendulum traverses. The first of them is easily do-able, and we traverse three metres above the Big Sur ledge to reach a huge, wafer-thin yet compact flake. To begin with we hesitate before trusting ourselves to it but there is no other possibility. It sounds excitingly hollow but it does at least manage to hold our weight and thus shades in yet another grey area on our sketched topo.

The next pendulum is a different matter, however. We search and search. Our hopes fade. Yet again a big question mark hangs over the Free Right Side project; the natural continuation leftwards into the big dihedral system is the missing link. We pendulum backwards and forwards, examine the tiniest details of the rock face, spend hours trying to find the solution that must lie hidden somewhere. We search in vain. For the time being it looks like the end; the link to the pitches above seems blocked. We both feel that this section will be the one that tests our motivation to the limit.

imaginable. After a certain period of adjustment we feel perfectly at home in this vertical environment; more secure, even, than on *terra firma*. But this effect can be deceptive. It conceals an enormous danger, for the seriousness of the situation must not be forgotten for even a single second. A fall of 500 metres would be sufficient to ensure that practically nothing remained of a human body on the ground below. And yet still we love living in this turned-around world. It brings a heightened awareness, a more intense level of consciousness, and grants us a feeling that only we can experience.

This special El Cap Big Wall experience is

Ray Jardine would have had no problem with it, to be sure – a few blows with the chisel and the passage would be climbable. For us, however, the rules are different. We will use only what Nature provides, and we will accept this impossible section for what it is. The real art lies in making the best of the situation. So we search for a way out.

Eight metres diagonally below we discover a

especially the nerve-racking monotony of drilling. The aggression caused by the brain-numbing tedium of hitting the drill bit at least speeds up the process. "You-shit-get-in-there!" – every syllable a hammer blow.

This is my sixth bolt today and I am wasted, my hands swollen and stained black by the aluminium. I look like a baker's apprentice, hair and face white and pasty from the granite dust that

◆ PROBLEMS ARE ONLY THERE TO BE SOLVED

no-hands rest, from where a shallow depression in the granite arches leftwards to the start of the 90 degree dihedral. It looks hard, but if a solution to our dilemma exists, then this is it. We place the necessary belay and protection bolts, yet our motivation for the work involved, up to now fired by our free climbing ideals, has sunk to its lowest ebb. Today everything is just too much for us,

even crunches between my teeth. If one of those Valley tourists were to ask me now why I do all this I would be lost for an answer.

Alexander is totally k.o., mainly because of this insurmountable barrier at the second pendulum. The vision of a totally free ascent of the Right Side has been shattered because of three lousy metres of blank granite. Three tiny matchstick edges would suffice for us to forge a link across the shallow granite arch. The hiss of the beer can and a deep swig brings new thoughts, abstruse ideas as to how we might free climb the eight-metre abseil section. Perhaps an eight-metre jump down onto the big jug at the no-hands rest, belayed on a slack ten-metre length of rope? Even if it worked it would mean at the very least a dislocated shoulder, and there is no way a free ascent would be worth that.

Alexander then develops an idea about how to free climb these eight metres – as a team. Problems are only there to be solved and our solution is freshly minted from Alexander's collection of ideas. The next morning we begin with the first test run. The preparations go as follows: Alexander ties off the rope on the stance, but leaves the rope slack enough so as not to weight the belay. He then gets hold of a good edge and stabilizes his position with two little smears. A 15-metre length of rope hangs from my brother's climbing harness. I have clipped my abseil device, a Gri-Gri, into this rope. It works like this: Alexander becomes a 'living abseil anchor', using only muscle power to hold my body weight, while I rap down the first four metres to a little ledge as fast as possible, where I take the weight off the rope. Alexander shakes

The big roof of the Black Cave, 5.13b/X–, a real speciality pitch, 'scary' and 'spacy', as the Americans say

out, chalks up, takes another deep breath and gives me a sign that he is ready. A little later I am standing at the belay, eight metres lower than Alexander, at the start of the next pitch. A crazy idea, but it works. It may well be rather unusual but, strictly speaking, we have done the section 'free as a team' ... Whether this 'manpowered rappel', as a free version of an otherwise impossible section, is a work of genius, completely insane or just banal is of no interest to us – our teamwork was at least better than Jardine's rape. We shift our gaze upwards, to where we hope to find the last hold of our route. The motivation is back. We are cooking with gas again.

We climb the next pitch and christen the nondescript rib in the sea of golden-yellow granite The Royal Arch. This pitch is not only fantastic climbing, unique even – at 5.13 it is also one of the hardest so far.

We are getting closer and closer to the spooky black roof above us. Alexander cleans the lichen from the Black Dihedral, searching for the best nut placements and marking them with a strip of finger tape. We leave nothing to chance. We memorize each and every move on the wall, and every piece of gear too. Every placement is noted down on a piece of paper.

Fifteen metres below the Black Cave we have to make a rightward deviation away from the original line, as the first roof looks too problematic. The variation does have its price however. The rock below the massive belt of roofs has obviously never seen water and the quality is correspondingly bad. These 20 metres are a real gravel pit, the rock comes down to meet you. From the rock quality point of view it is a heap of rubble up here, 'the worst case on El Cap'.

On the topo the rock hereabouts is described as 'loose and rotten', the nightmare of every Big-Waller. Yet it still offers the best and easiest way of reaching the heart of the Black Cave. We call the nightmarishly loose rock scenery Rotten Island. It takes a huge amount of cleaning work in order to sort out a climbable line through the rubble. At the end of Operation Rotten Island we have a rucksack full of rocks. We wait until nightfall before sending them off on their journey down to the Valley.

Alexander is now busy trying to unlock the secret of the Black Cave. This, we believe, is the last real obstacle on the way to the summit. The first section of the double roof combination obviously presents him with no great problems. At the top of the dihedral he bridges out wide, almost doing the splits, and places a whole nest of good gear, before shimmying up somehow between the twin roofs into a little slot in the middle of the

Alexander on Galapagos pitch, 5.13c/X–

roof and a no-hands rest in an absolutely mad position.

The remaining six metres to the belay look hard, however, and the protection is atrocious. A Friend rammed behind a hollow, clapped-out flake merely serves to calm the nerves, the next knife blade is bendy and rusty into the bargain and might just about hold his body weight but in the event of a fall it propably wouldn't even slow him down. An angle, sawn-off to abcut two centimetres, pokes out of a shallow hole on the lip of the roof. This dubious piece is the last pseudo protection for a cross-through move in a position of breathtaking exposure. A bolt would, of course, be appropriate here, essential even, but to place a bolt in the most spectacular place on the whole of the North America Wall would not only represent a violation of the rules of the Yosemite way of climbing, it would also show a distinct lack of respect for the boldness of the first ascentionist.

Alexander tries the cross-through move several times. Again and again he down-climbs and cautiously sits on the exceptionally dubious piece. As the belayer this means I have to pay out an exact amount of rope as he climbs and take in carefully each time he retreats, quickly paying out about 20 centimetres at the last possible moment to ensure that there is no jerk on the top piece of

Endurance Corner,
5.12a/VIII+, a textbook corner crack

gear. Alexander rests for ten minutes, then gives it another go and makes it past the cross-through move. He can not risk falling now under any circumstances. He swings his feet up and left over the lip of the roof and makes a controlled grab for the next holds. He is now three metres above the sawn-off angle, with another metre to go to the stance. As he disappears from sight beyond the edge of the roof I can only wait, either for the sharp jerk as Alexander sails through the air in a wide arc, ripping out all the bits of protection in the roof like a zip-fastener, or for his shout of release as he reaches the belay.

He shouts, and luckily it is a shout of joy . . . this bloody guy has got nerves like steel wire. Years ago, during the first ascent, Royal Robbins described Tom Pratt's lead of the Black Cave as 'the most spectacular lead in the history of American climbing'. Now, 34 years later, Alexander has turned this roof into a work of free climbing art, involving cross-through moves, dynos, powerful lock-offs, hand-traversing with legs dangling completely free of the rock.

At this point on the route there is no longer any ground beneath your feet. The climber must complete the gymnastic sequence 'in total space' with 600 metres of fresh air under his backside and a two-centimetre-long sawn-off angle for protection. Thanks to Alexander we have now regained full contact with the rock and the way ahead is clear to the upper part of the wall.

For three more days we are busy trying to find the best and easiest line through the Cyclop's Eye and the Headwall. The last question mark, the overhang barring the exit from the Cyclop's Eye, succumbs to an elegant detour. A roof split by a chimney crack leads off to the left. Beneath the roof is the crucial foothold, a thin dinnerplate flake stuck to the face that looks like a dolphin's head. We christen this stubborn pitch The Dolphin. Finally, the last bolt sinks into the granite and we climb the last pitch.

Sweaty, covered in scratches, and encrusted with grit and grime, we sit at the top of our route. We have taken a full two weeks to solve the puzzle. We have created a free-climbing link between the first hold on the first pitch and the last hold on the last pitch, incorporating a tricksome solution to an unclimbable passage. We often climbed alongside existing routes but again and

defined by finger strength, balance, the interplay between muscle power and mind control, physical and mental stamina.

Everything has been prepared, each pitch stored in our heads. After two rest days in the Valley, with leisurely breakfasts in the Cafeteria and river bathing in the Merced, our batteries are fully recharged. All the little injuries have healed, the swellings on our fingers have subsided. Nothing more stands in the way of our first redpoint attempt on El Niño. Even the weather forecast gives us the green light for the next three days. Our planned style of ascent is derived from traditional Alpine mountaineering climbing as a rope of two and switching leads but only attributing the label 'team redpoint' to the ascent once all the pitches have been climbed free with no falls by both partners. The question of whether it is better from a style and performance point of view for one person or both members of the team to make a redpoint ascent is a difficult one to answer. With a team ascent a pitch can only be considered done when the second has also followed the pitch with no falls; the team thus forms a single unit in which team spirit, trust, identical levels of performance and a one hundred per cent dedication to the cause play a fundamental role. Compare this with an individual redpoint ascent. Here, the main feature is the higher demand made on the leading ability of one person. At the top of each pitch the

 THIS BLOODY GUY HAS GOT NERVES LIKE STEEL WIRE

again we were forced to quit the tenuous hairline cracks, impossible for us free climbers, and seek out our own free variations.

The resultant hybrid is a mixture of Continental Drift, our own variations and New Jersey Turnpike on the lower third of the wall, followed by sections of North America Wall and many new variations again almost to the top, with the last two pitches of the route Sea of Dreams. It is a patchwork quilt of classic and modern techno-routes supplemented by our own creations which, when viewed as a whole, has the status of a new route. It marks a new direction in the technoland of El Capitan. Or, metaphorically speaking, a new, fresh wind is blowing over the West Coast of the North American continent, bringing with it a significant change in climate. This climate shift is caused by the Pacific Ocean current 'El Niño' and the forecast is that henceforth climbing will be

leader fixes the rope and can then concentrate on the next pitch, while the second, his belay partner, jumars up the fixed line. The resultant pause in the procedings means that the overall achievement of both styles of ascent is pretty much balanced out.

We are all fired up and ready to go. At 9 o'clock in the morning we are at the start of the route, ready to give it our all – until Alexander realizes that he has left his harness in the car. The initial fire subsides as he, normally the perfectionist of our team and now the victim of his own carelessness, berates his stupidity and our start is delayed by one and a half hours.

The Black Dike and Missing Link are despatched first go, but we stumble on the Galapagos pitch. Alexander has already redpointed the thing but when seconding the pitch my rock boot slips off a foot change on a smear. Shit! I can't afford to do that again. After a short rest at the belay I set off up the Galapagos again feeling every bit as nervous as I would if I were leading it. It is the responsibility towards your partner that causes this feeling and sharpens the concentration, even when seconding. This time the foot change works and a little while later the first crux, the three consecutive 5.13 pitches, are behind us. We continue up to the Calaveras Ledges and rap down the fixed ropes to the Valley in the late afternoon.

The next day, carrying some provisions for a bivouac, we jumar back up to the previous day's high point and climb the section from the Calaveras Ledges to Big Sur in two hours. After a short break we set off again. We both manage M & M Flake, Manpowered Rappel, Royal Arch, Endurance Corner and Black Dihedral at the first attempt. Then we fix the ropes and abseil back down to our camp on Big Sur.

Day three, and the last big hurdle still lies ahead, the Black Cave. In the morning, after our rather meagre breakfast, we climb this black crypt first go. The rest is pure routine. We are so deep into our climbing that we fail to notice the black storm clouds brewing in the sky. At the end of the difficulties, a hundred metres short of the top, a light rain begins to fall. We hit the gas pedal, total speed-climbing. If the storm hits us here we will have no chance of climbing the easier-angled exit slabs and will have to spend a further night on the wall with no protection at all from the elements.

"On belay, when you're ready!"

"Quick, take in, climbing!"

We climb as fast as we possibly can without being irresponsible about it. We are in luck; the storm rains itself out somewhere over Half Dome. Towards evening we top out. We celebrate our success with a handshake that spells release. More than 30 pitches lie below us, our hands are in tatters. Suddenly the heavens open and it starts to bucket down with rain.

Wild, exposed, overhanging and yet only VII:

Thomas on the frightening chimney of the Dolphin, 5.10c/VII

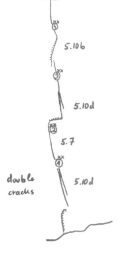

THE EAR
5.8 chimney
5.10c
5.10b
5.10a
5.10a
5.8
chimney
HOLLOW FLAKE LEDGE
5.9 O.W.
8"
3rd
5.10d
MAMMOUTH TERRASSES
5.11b
5.10b
HEART LEDGES
5.7
5.7
Half Dollar
5.10c
5.8
5.11a
5.11a
5.10b
5.10d
5.7
double cracks
5.10d

HARDWARE FOR FREERIDER:

nuts
1 ea. TCU 0.5, TCU 0.75
1 ea. CAM 0.5, CAM 0.75, CAM 4
2 ea. CAM 1, CAM 2, CAM 3
1 "BIG DADDY" (7" or 8")

In the summer of 1998 the climbing scene in the Valley was turned on its head as the Gladiators of the Vertical pushed back the boundaries of the possible. Meanwhile the danger, the calculated risk that these people knew they were taking, hung like the Sword of Damocles above their heads. They did not always survive.

Dan Osman kept on improving on his record for a free fall on a climbing rope until finally the rope broke and not much of him remained on the ground below. For someone who always erred on the side of caution, or so he thought, it must have been a stupid oversight, it was perhaps being too lazy at the gear check before the jump, that cost him his life. His personal best, a 300-metre free fall, will not be bettered very quickly. The record stands, but the Valley has one crazy guy less.

Dean Potter and his climbing partner José Pereyra have broken five records in Speed Climbing, the climbing of a route in as short a time as possible. Using every technical trick in their repertoire they raced up the Big Walls of Yosemite, climbing the 35 pitch, thousand-metres-long Salathé in a total time of 8 hours 51 minutes. It was an outstanding new speed record but one which stood for less than a week. The old speed kings Hans Florine and Steve Schneider reclaimed the crown for the fastest ascent of this classic route by shaving a further 45 minutes off the best time. No problem, Dean and José thought. Two days later they replied with a utopian 7 hours 33 minutes. Dean and José smiled, that's life . . .

The speed rush reached its climax a little later with Dean's speed solo of the North West Face of Half Dome in 4 hours 17 minutes, shattering the old

the speed comes as a result of calmly executed and fluid moves. To add to the challenge, there is the stipulation that a free, speed ascent can only be regarded as valid when the route is redpointed.

In 1996 I made an attempt on the El Capitan free climbing record – still held by Lynn Hill, who climbed the Nose in 23 hours – via the Salathé. It was unsuccessful. Now, two years later, we are about to give it another go.

As a by product of his visit to the Valley in 1995 Alexander had left a new variation on the Salathé, which he soloed and which cleverly avoids the actual crux of the Salathé, the Headwall.

It provides a first class option for a one-day free

◆ THE ALARM CLOCK SHOWS 2 O'CLOCK. WE ARE READY FOR TAKE-OFF AND TRIMMED FOR SPEED

best time of 21 hours. Apart from a few sections, he climbed the route unroped, trusting only his equipment and his climbing abilities – in true gladiatorial style. How much more speed can a man take?

The mixture of speed and free climbing is just another form of thrill seeking or vertical high. The rules are the same, a race for the best time, but the execution is fundamentally different. Whereas the speed climber will make a hectic grab for the *in situ* gear (the main thing is not to waste any time) and climb the route any old how, the speed free-climber must carry out co-ordinated and controlled sequences of moves. In the end,

ascent of El Cap! Back in '95 Alexander lacked both the time and the partner for his attempt and since the 'Freerider in a day' project would have been easy pickings for somebody, he kept absolutely quiet about the existence of this variation. Until now. Now we are back, this time there are two of us, and we are very motivated after our successful free ascent of the 'Right side'. We are well up for it – 'Freerider', team ascent, redpoint, in one day, a 1000-metre trip through the El Cap desert. The difficulties nowhere exceed grade IX and the route is now well within the capabilities of a large number of climbers. Perhaps it will become the free climbing classic

5.12c

5.12a

SOUS LE TOIT

5.10d

THE BLOCK

5.10d

A1

5.12d(?)   5.12d

5.11d   5.12a

5.10d

5.6 chimney

5.11a

EL
CAP
SPIRE   5.7 chimney

5.10a
O.W.

5.10d
O.W.   5.13c

5.13d

5.12b

5.10d
O.W.

5.12a

THE EAR

of the year 2000. If Ray Jardine had only known . . .

The preparations: we know from a team who have only recently climbed the Salathé that there are three litres of water stashed behind a block on the Sous Le Toit ledge 700 metres up the route. That must be enough and anyway we reckon on finding other drinkable stuff on the bivi ledges.

The gear is reduced down as far as possible; anything superfluous would just be unnecessary ballast. It is a little rack for a big route: ten Friends of various sizes, eight Stoppers, seven quick draws, eight extra carabiners and the Big Daddy, an oversized Friend to protect the monster crack below El Cap Spire. We will climb on a 70-metre 8.8-mm rope. It is very light and by taking a longer rope we hope to be able to run some of the pitches together and save ourselves some time.

The evening before the attempt we check all the gear one more time, assessing whether each piece of equipment is absolutely necessary, and manage to reduce the rack by a further two Stoppers and a Friend in order to save weight. The rest of the gear is prepared in a similarly painstaking way. We slip a couple of muesli bars into the loops on the chalkbag where we usually hang old toothbrushes, used to brush off the holds, and fill the bag itself to the brim with chalk. A roll of tape is pressed into service as a first aid kit; the headtorches are fitted with fresh batteries for the night-time climbing action. This time Alexander makes 100% sure that he has packed both his rock shoes and his harness in his rucksack.

The alarm clock shows 2 o' clock. We are ready for take-off and trimmed for speed.

3:00 We are at the start of the Salathé, where we stuff the trekking shoes, fleeces and lined trousers into our rucksack – that stays here. We tank up again on mineral drink. Alexander laces his rock shoes.

3:31: Alexander sets off, climbing by the light of the headtorch. We climb the first eleven pitches – the Free Blast – in total darkness.

7:00 Sunrise. We are on the Mammoth Ledges, where we find a plastic bottle with water, quench our thirst, clip the headtorches to our harness and set off again. Hollow Flake. The Ear.

9:30 We arrive at the start of the monster crack.

11:00 We both sit for a moment on El Cap Spire, exhausted after the struggle in the off-width. The crack has cost us valuable time and energy.

13:30 The Block, a good place for a rest, time for the first muesli bar. We have done the hardest pitch now and are still on course for success but there are still some very hard and strenuous crack and dihedral pitches to come. Time is getting short; only five hours of daylight left. We keep on going fast, can't afford to waste any more time.

14:00 Sous Le Toit – we find the water, at last. The fluid freshens up our reserves of strength.

15:30 Stance below the Great Roof, leading onto the Headwall. This is the start of the superb, exposed 10-metre leftwards traverse to the Round Table Bivy, first discovered and climbed by Alexander in 1995. Our muscles are cramping up more and more frequently; the skin on our fingers is worn through and sensitive, preventing any powerful fingery moves; the soles of our feet are burning; but willpower keeps driving us onwards and upwards.

17:00 Four pitches to the top and we are still on course for the redpoint. The second muesli bar has long since ceased to exist; the energy reserves are depleted. Just 1½ hours of daylight left. It's going to be a close run thing.

18:56 It is dark. We top out on Freerider. 37 pitches, 5.12d, in 15 hours and 25 minutes, redpoint, as a team.

We are tired, snuggle down into the sleeping bags we left after El Niño and enjoy the peace and quiet without having to worry about the time. The next morning we descend the East Ledges, barefoot, since our shoes are down at the start of the route. Saves weight, you see.

THE FREERIDER

THE HEADWALL
SALATHÉ

ROUND
TABLE
BIVY

5.5

5.10b
O.W.

5.10d

5.11d

5.12a

LONG LEDGE

THE ROOF

Alexander leading the 33rd pitch of Freerider, 5.11d/VIII

OGRE

THE MAN EATER

Of the 30 or so expeditions to this mountain only one has so far been successful. No one has yet reached the summit via the sunlit South Buttress in the middle of the photo. The Ogre, 7285m, Karakorum/Pakistan, 1999
Alexander Huber

The Ogre – the man-eating monster – has earned its name. Piece by piece it eats us up, gnaws at our psyche. It demands everything from us, just as it did from the first ascentionists in 1977 when, only a few metres below the summit, Doug Scott

broke both of his legs, the weather suddenly turned nasty, Chris Bonington fell and broke several ribs and then contracted pneumonia. After a week-long desperate fight for survival the Ogre finally let them escape, but not before it had tested them to the very limit of their endurance. It was this dramatic first ascent that made the mountain famous.

The Ogre is not an 8000er and thus there has never been a headlong rush to climb it. Yet with every failed attempt that the Ogre has added to its collection over the years the mountain has grown in stature, a precious stone that the extreme mountaineer seeks to grasp. In the 22 years since it was first climbed more than 15 expeditions have failed; the chances of success are small, yet for us that is exactly where the attraction lies – we are going to try anyway.

But not by the route taken by the first ascent team. Their route, via the West Col and the West Ridge, is threatened by séracs for much of its length, a risk that can not be calculated and one which, for us, seems too great – even this mountain is not worth that!

Thomas on the steep first third of the Buttress. We climbed the original aid pitches free (to grade VIII), but used fixed ropes thereafter as time was an issue

We have decided to go for the South Buttress of the Ogre. This prominent jutting prow of rock, is at once impressive and on first appearances awe-inspiring but closer inspection reveals it to be appealing due to its very exposure as it is safe from stone fall and avalanches. The Buttress itself was actually first climbed 15 years ago by the French pair Fine and Vauquet but they were caught out by bad weather high on the mountain and failed to reach the summit. In 1997 Jan and his partner were the last team to attempt the South Buttress of the Ogre. They reached the top of the thousand-metre pillar in only six days, faster than their predecessors, but were also surprised by a sudden worsening in the weather and did not reach the summit.

In the tactical game of climbing the Ogre it is the weather, on top of the personal skills required, that is the decisive element. We consider our tactics – put simply, we must be faster than the bad weather. We hope to reach the summit from Base Camp in

◆ INACTIVITY WEARS ME OUT

only four days – two days for the Buttress, the third day for the big ice field to the foot of the summit tower, then summiting and returning to the top of the South Buttress on day four. From there we would be able to descend even in bad weather. Four successive days of fine weather – that is all we really need for the summit.

The month of July somehow slips by and we have had only five days of useful weather, but never more than three in succession. If the general weather situation does not improve we will be unable to mount even a single attempt on the Ogre. 30 days of sitting around at Base Camp and even I start questioning the sense of it all. I feel like I have never in my life been so unproductive. Doing nothing wears me out. You sit in the big

communal tent at Base Camp, zip open the window and throw handfuls of money out . . . and subsequently question what earthly use the whole thing could be. You need not really think about it at all, of course, since you already know the answer – frustration. It can no longer be hidden; it is writ large on everyone's face.

Climbing the biggest mountains in the world is a paradoxical thing. Up on the mountain you long for the calm and security of Base Camp but once you are back at Base it is not long before you start getting restless again; you want to go back up. They are two mutually exclusive worlds and no matter which world I find myself in I always want to be somewhere other than where I am. One, two, maybe three days of doing nothing is often the nicest thing there is. But then the restlessness begins to grow and every day it gets stronger and stronger. It is our society that shapes us. It decrees that there must be something wrong with you if you do nothing for a long time. You are a useless good-for-nothing layabout! We climbers often think of ourselves as the wild ones – and yet we too, without exception, sit in the prison of society even if it seems as if we are spending three months totally cut off from it. We will always return there; the expedition is not an escape, merely a brief release from society's confines during which we are obliged to conduct ourselves in accordance with society's rules. Now Base Camp is our prison, with civilisation clawing at its invisible walls.

"What is it that is keeping me here?"

"Who is it that is keeping me waiting?"

"Oh yes, the Ogre."

To say that I had almost forgotten about it would be untrue, however. Like the Sword of Damocles it hangs above my head, weighing heavily down upon my psyche, which attempts to save itself by suppressing all thoughts. We have been waiting for the Ogre for weeks now. Although we still have two more weeks – enough time to give us a realistic chance of summiting – I still find it hard to believe we will be successful. I have somehow lost the feeling that we will manage to do it.

This time it never really got going right from the start, even the preparations for the expedition were born under a bad sign. A week before the start of the expedition Thomas injured his knee. The gear arrived in Pakistan ten days late. What were we meant to do in the meantime? We played cards until we were sick of it, hung around the hotel and ran backwards and forwards to the

British Airways office. Then there was the phone call from the German Embassy warning travellers that the conflict in Kashmir was about to escalate. No one at the Embassy, or anywhere else for that matter, seemed to know where the conflict would lead or how far India and Pakistan would be prepared to go but in any event Skardu was likely to be an attractive target for India's efforts if the situation were to become critical. It had to

be really, since there was no other place in the Pakistani Kashmir region where large aircraft could be landed and Skardu is also a garrison town. According to information from the German Embassy an additional brigade was already on the way there, with more to follow should the conflict escalate further.

Did we really want to go there? We had to; it was the only way to get to our mountain. Skardu is the gateway to the Central Karakorum; anyone heading into the heart of the highest mountains in Pakistan has to pass through here. However, the capital of the province of Baltisan stayed safe and we had no problems on the journey in. In the Latok region we would be safe too; we would be about a hundred kilometres from the war zone there and the high chain of mountains between are luckily still impassable for a troop of foot soldiers. But what about on the way back? At first, no one could give us any guarantees about how the situation would look at the end of August. It was still three months away and the war season in Kashmir had only just begun. The snow had started melting in the war zones, some of which were 5000 metres up, and the fighting had been getting harder, more bitter and bloodier than ever. We devoted a great deal of time to the subject of 'the war'. The walk-in and the time spent at Base Camp would certainly not present any problems. But what would happen if the way back was blocked and the conflict had by then spread as far as Skardu? We sounded out the options in the case of an emergency. The border with China was only 30 kilometres away from Base Camp. It would be possible to get to China in six days over the 5400-metre pass of the Lukpe La. No problem at all from a mountaineering point of view – the only question that remained was what the Chinese would have to say on the matter. I had obtained the number of the German Embassy in Peking – bought a ticket for our escape route as it were – and hoped this would be enough ammunition for any eventuality.

It is 10 o' clock in the morning and I am standing in the freight hall again. Finally there is a good sign; our coveted items of gear are lying there, our equipment is complete. The long journey into Base Camp lies before us. Once there we pitch the tents, sort the equipment and prepare the climbing gear.

The weather is perfect. It is looking good, Thomas's knee is no longer troubling him, let the Ogre game commence.

The link to the upper third of the Buttress is formed by an easy-angled arête, at the end of which is an ideal place for our Portaledge Camp

The war. For two weeks now we have been hearing the dull rumble of heavy artillery in the battle zone. It was almost to be expected that the religious fanaticism of the two states of Pakistan and India would not contribute to a quick solution to the problems and that there would be massive battles – but actually to hear the weapons being employed with your own ears is a nerve racking thing. I get really mad when the Pakistanis answer our fears with just a "no problem" or a "like every year" or shift the blame for the conflict elsewhere with their "Pakistan army no fighting, only Mujahedeen." I only need to read the newspaper to find out what is going on. Ismail listens to

On the upper third of the Buttress: vertical granite, ice-choked cracks, this is grade VI free climbing at 6000 metres

122

the news every day – he is concerned about his younger brother, who is a soldier in the Pakistani army.

On 15th June a mail runner arrives with bad news. Ismail's brother has fallen on the Kashmir front. Ismail himself leaves us that same day to return to his family of ten, whose head he now is. And for days now heavy clouds have been hanging over the peaks of the Karakorum; five days of miserable

weather yet again. We are more than fed up with it all; the long days of sitting around at Base Camp are getting to us. To be up on the mountain would mean distraction; it would help to get our thoughts back in order. But the general weather situation is simply bad and as long as there is no change we will not be able to count on the four settled days we need.

I look up at the Ogre; it is still there, as always, but with every passing day it gets harder for me to see the way to the top. I do not want to let a single chance slip by, for sure, and that is why I am still here at all. But in spite of this I have already dismissed the idea of the summit. Like a cat that sits in front of a mouse hole for hours on end, waiting for its prey, I sit for weeks at Base Camp, waiting stoically and patiently for my own chance to pounce. If the prey fails to show itself the cat moves on. If the summit of the Ogre does not come into my field of vision I too will move on. The hunt will have failed. Nothing unusual for the cat; nothing unusual on the Ogre.

But the hunt goes on. I will return – not necessarily to this same mountain but certainly to mountaineering, to these frozen giants, to the tons of moraine rubble, the séracs, the avalanches, the heat and the cold. Mountaineering on the highest mountains in the world is no pleasure; the mountain adventure gains its fascination only by a very circuitous route. When you are at home you wish you were out and about in the wild, savage mountains. The fascination is based upon the very human character trait of wanting to do exactly what it is impossible to do at any given time. That is why we climbers are so often envied. Everyone who is completely tied in to society, with a regular career, responsibilities and a family, looks upon our independence with jealousy as we pack our things yet again and journey out into the world for two or three months at a time.

That is exactly where I am now sitting, at the end of the world, independent again – no telephone, no radio, no post, surrounded by moraine rubble, rock and ice. Right at this moment, however, I would far sooner be sitting in a beer garden, meeting friends, enjoying a green and warm summer, swimming in crystal clear mountain lakes, touching warm rock. . . .

I do not really want to climb this mountain in front of me any more. I no longer want to expose myself to all the fears up there on the mountain – the fear of being high up on the Ogre with the weather

breaking; the fear of sliding down the South Face on a snow slab avalanche; the fear of the séracs, of stone fall, of the altitude; the fear of making a mistake.

To hold the brief, short-lived moments of success in our memory are the dreams for which we climb on the high mountains again and again. This time, however, the success belongs to the 'others' – success on Broad Peak, success on Gasherbrum II, success on Trango Tower – as again and again we hear the reports of successful expeditions on the radio. With a certain amount of envy we hear of those who have already summited – if we had chosen an easier objective we would already have our peak in the bag as well. But over and over again it was the same mountains where the successes were being celebrated, big-name objectives with maximum probability of success. As I gaze at the Ogre the envy quickly passes as I remind myself why it was this one that I had chosen – because it has an extremely low success rate; because I do not wish to share Base Camp with a hundred others; because on our mountain we are alone and do not have to follow in the well-trodden tracks of others; because it is a real and pure challenge.

27th July. Yesterday at sunset it suddenly cleared so we decided to set off during the night. For the third time we go up to the Camp on the Buttress at 6000 metres. The route to Advance Base Camp, through the ice fall, up the couloir and then the first few pitches of the Buttress, is slowly getting on my nerves. I can't stand the sight of it any more. Eventually I am sitting with Thomas on the Portaledge with Jan and Toni on the Ledge next to us. Again it is the same phenomenon – I feel at home on the Ledge, I feel good. Feeling calm and relaxed, I look forward to what tomorrow has in

winds high on the mountain, at about 6500 metres. We decide not to set off at 2.00 am but to wait until daybreak. The morning does not promise good weather for the next few days and since we do not want to waste our energies on a hopeless jaunt we decide to put everything on one last attempt and descend, for the third time, without ever having tried to make a real push for the top. Jan, however, decides not only go down but to call it a day. He tried the South Buttress back in 1997 and has invested too much energy for too little reward; he has had quite enough of this mountain.

The last attempt. The weather is getting even worse. For four nights in succession we get up at 2.00 am; the clouds are hanging low. Thomas, Toni and I set off three more times up the Ogre, each time in floods of snow and rain from the glacier. Twice we turn back before Advance Base but the third time we push on through, since mathematically speaking this is the last chance we

FEELING CALM AND RELAXED, I LOOK FORWARD TO WHAT TOMORROW HAS IN STORE FOR US

store for us: 13 pitches of classic free climbing, not overly difficult but we want – need – to get it done in a day. We will not be taking the Portaledges with us, which means we will be forced to bivi on the top of the Buttress. A haul bag and three heavy rucksacks have to be carried up there and this means that the climbing becomes a secondary issue; the dominant problem is the logistics of getting all the gear up there as fast as possible. During the night the cirrus cloud in evidence throughout the day gets thicker, with extreme

will get. We start up the Buttress in spindrift and strong wind, with ice-encrusted ropes and the wind whipping around the edge of the buttress. If it gets any worse we will not even be able to get to the camp on the Buttress to fetch the gear down. We are now finished with the Ogre. Finally. At last. 5th August. We can count ourselves lucky that we are able to clear the Buttress Camp and thus withdraw without material loss. The Ogre project is over now and Toni follows Jan back down into the valley. Thomas and I will have another five days to wait until the porters arrive – another chance for success on Latok IV at least, after having to turn back a month ago, when still climbing as a team of four, due to the difficulties I had getting acclimatized.

From Base Camp it is a twelve kilometre walk-in across the Baintha Lukpar Glacier, followed by the converge to form a steepening couloir; only 200 metres separate us from the col on the summit plateau. Time to start belaying. The diarrhoea is stressful; I am dehydrated and totally worn out. Thomas, by contrast, is bursting with energy and now takes over the job of leading the 60° steep couloir, giving me, as second man, maximum

◆ ICE FIELDS AS STEEP AS THE SPIDER ON THE EIGER

South West Face itself and a height gain of 2100 metres – a long way and one which we intend to accomplish without a camp in a single day. My performance is hampered by an attack of diarrhoea so we want to start out very early and take things a bit slower. At eleven o' clock at night we set off and stagger across the rubble-strewn glacier heading for the start of the South West Face of Latok IV.

Ice fields as steep as the Spider on the North Face of the Eiger. We climb everything unroped; it is the only way to get the whole ascent and descent done in a single day. We have hardly any gear with us: a rope, a stove, one canister of gas, eight muesli bars apiece for provisions, otherwise nothing. In the Himalayas this is the only way to do big distances in a short time. High up, the extensive ice fields

security despite my increasing exhaustion.

The last few metres into the col drag on and on, I have to fight for every metre. When I reach the summit plateau I am totally spent. Exhausted, I lie down in the snow. It is 12 o' clock. Black clouds all around us. We should really be on the way back down by now, for the ice fields on the South West Face get more dangerous in the afternoon hours, with stone fall and small snow avalanches. It is too late. I would need too long for the last few metres to the summit and the descent would be too dangerous as a result. I give up. I leave the summit to Thomas; he is still moving fast. In this way we will have a more or less acceptable amount of time left to begin the descent. Thomas sets off climbing. He has decided to go for the South Summit since it is more easily and rapidly accessible from the col

Spindrift and bitter cold, ice-encrusted ropes and the wind whipping around the edge of the buttress

Latok IV with the South West Face

Shortly before the summit plateau at 6400 metres:
a steep bulge gives vertical ice climbing

fall, avalanche, collapsing snow bridges over gaping bergschrunds – it was a dangerous descent, a calculated risk on our part but without them it is impossible to achieve any really worthwhile objectives in the Himalayas.

Home at last! The many tortuous days of inactivity are now a thing of the past. Now it is all hectic and stress; a crass difference.

I landed two days ago. Three months in foreign parts, cut off, in hiding, while back home everything was piling up. Now the dam breaks and the pressure of civilisation hits me with full force. I have difficulty readjusting and look around for something to hold on to. Thomas has that already, his son Elias has been waiting for him for weeks. But where are my friends? No one about? Oh yes,

and suddenly, much earlier than expected, he tops out. The featureless snow mushrooms adorning the twin peaks of Latok IV are deceptive; we had expected another 200 metres of height gain but it turns out to be no more than 50 and after ten minutes Thomas is on the top.

"If that is all it is I can manage it too," I think and immediately start to feel better! I pull myself together, helped by Thomas, who is back with me again and using all his energy to fire me up. "It's no more than 50 metres, you can do that! The other summit is a bit higher but we don't need to worry about that now. I'll sort out the first abseil – and you go for it."

An hour before sunset we reach safe ground again and a further two hours – a total of 22 hours climbing without a break – sees us back at Base Camp. Of course we were too late descending and had to take the dangerous bits in stages, front-pointing down at high speed. Exhaustion, stone

On the South West Face of Latok IV,
shortly before reaching the col,
the link to the upper section of the Face

that's right, it is August, holiday time! This time there is no success to fall back on and I become aware of how hard failure can be. While still at Base Camp I had accepted and come to terms with not getting to the summit of the Ogre. After the endless weeks of waiting I was even happy finally to evacuate the mountain and put an end to the

AND STILL WE HAVE THE HUNGER

claustrophobic hanging around waiting for a chance to go for the top. But with every homeward step I realized more and more what was waiting for me and what I really needed now was to relax and recover.

Success would have compensated much, if not all of this; the euphoria would have seen me through the lack of an opportunity to recover. But the way things are, every step back towards my daily routine merely serves to demonstrate that I have not been successful. To come back with the summit means you have gained energy, despite all the hardships. Without the summit you first fall into a deep valley of depression on your return home. You are drained dry, at the end of your tether, but you have to battle on regardless and work through the backlog caused by your three month absence.

And still we have the hunger. We do not climb mountains just because they are there. We climb mountains because we want to stand on the top. Not reaching the top weighs all the more heavily because it is a job you have not completed. And the summit itself? Well, for a brief moment we leave our footprints on the highest point of a mountain. We stand right at the top . . . but we have also finished the job we set out to do, we are free again. This makes us prisoners of ourselves and of our unfinished business.

I hear again the soft splashing of the stream at Base Camp, the distant roar of the high-altitude storm; I feel the red granite of the Ogre, on which I climbed for just a few short hours. The Ogre is still unfinished business.

Experience is based upon memories of things already experienced and the intensive experience of having now to come to terms with this unfinished business will root itself deep in my conscience in the same way as success; as a positive result, a positive experience. The memory still hurts but already the old skin is starting to peel and the scar tissue starting to harden. The bottom line of the positive experience is measured in terms of maturity and the restlessness will soon begin again. Then it will be time to set off again and to return to those frozen giants.

The Ogre, as it appeared on the majority of days. Despite the fine weather, high altitude storms produce fascinating cloud formations above the summit

The mountaineer who has never failed has either never tried to do anything at the edge of being possible or has died young. Failure goes hand in hand with mountaineering, just like the cold on the eight-thousanders and the retreat in the snowstorm.

Which of the great alpinists has not failed on a mountain, failed again and again, failed despite the boldest of intentions? There was Walter Bonatti, for example, on K2; Chris Bonington who, together with Doug Scott, made the first successful ascent of the Ogre, on the Western Ridge of K2 and the North East Ridge of Everest; Christophe Profit on the South Face of Lhotse. Yet despite this they are still the ones who, through their successes as well as their failures, have defined mountaineering on the highest peaks of the world. Even George Leigh Mallory failed three times in succession attempting to conquer the highest mountain in the world and yet he is the one who, 75 years after his disappearance on the summit ridge, remains unforgotten. With his failure he became a legend, even more so than Hillary and Tensing, who were the first to step onto the Roof of the World in 1953.　　　　　R.M.

Reinhold Messner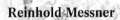

No, it is certainly not a scandal to fail on the Ogre. The central buttress of of this peak, which is so difficult to access, is compact and extremely difficult, and moreover the terrain is prone to avalanches and the route finding awkward. In other words, it is not a route best suited to bad weather conditions.

After the group of four from the Huber expedition had fixed the route as far as the middle section of the buttress, the climbers waited for their opportunity. They wanted to get to the summit and back from Base Camp in just four days and in 'alpine style'. But in the summer of 1999 the weather was never good for more than two days in succession and thus their hopes and chances were dashed. The two Huber brothers did however eventually manage to reach the southern summit of the six-thousander Latok IV – in a 22 hour non-stop push from Base Camp to the summit and back – but were unable to get onto any of the famous Ogre summits, that triple-peaked summit ridge that had remained unclimbed since 1977.

It was not a good summer in the Karakorum. During the many weeks at Base Camp, in addition to the noise of avalanches, there was the rumbling and roaring of the war nearby to contend with, as well as the noise of helicopters and aeroplanes. The border conflict between Pakistan and India had already made the approach journey difficult. Despite all this, however, Alexander and Thomas Huber did not regret their attempt. Failure is a part of extreme mountaineering too and in the end we learn a lot more from it than from a whole series of successes.

Will the Huber brothers return to the Ogre? Let's not ask them the question, for they will answer with their actions. In an age of empty announcements and headstands on the summit, the facts are more important to them than the empty actions of a few stars showing off to their fan club. What lengths will people go to to grab the attention of an uncritical public?

To stand right at the top may fill you with pride, yet to attempt the ascent via a difficult route is in every way a richer experience even when the summit is not reached. Who, today, does not know the empty gestures that turn the banal into something special, even on the mountain? In the end, however, they merely reveal the weakness of the players and further shatter that charisma which once was accorded mountaineering, like respect for the mountaineer. For even the star who does a headstand on the summit remains a mountaineer and the more important he thinks this will make him, the more ludicrous his actions seem. Thus in the end it will remain as it has always been – only exposure, difficulty and danger will be honoured, not the gag which demonstrates nothing but the small stature of the achievement.

One thing is certain: the Huber brothers will continue to climb their difficult routes in the big mountains. It is always more honourable to fail on something demanding than to race to the top of one of the prestigious peaks in the slipstream of a commercial expedition, via the easiest route, which has for ten years been prepared, rigged with safety equipment, sold out and which can still be done even when the weather is doubtful.

127

THOMAS AND ALEXANDER HUBER: "THE HUBER BROTHERS"

"Brüder haben ein Geblüte, selten aber ein Gemüte."

Friedrich von Logau's aphorism has been around for five times as long as the combined age of Thomas and Alexander – an old pearl of wisdom that has stood the test of time. The Baroque nobleman's observation is confirmed by the Huber Brothers. The secret of this well practised and powerful climbing team probably lies in their different characters and attitudes to life and the interplay between their opposing views.

And yet there is common ground, even in their characters: reliability, helpfulness, honesty are the family ties. Both are state-registered mountain guides and ski instructors as well as professional climbers. This book bears testimony to their outstanding skills as all-round mountaineers.

Alexander Huber

Alexander is the pragmatist with the phenomenal patience, the analytical planner (he is a physicist), the rationalist who pursues his goals with unsurpassed stubbornness. Born in 1968, he is the younger of the two brothers. He appraises and calculates every eventuality; sober, objective, outwardly unemotional.

Thomas Huber

Thomas, on the other hand, (b. 1966), is cast in a very different mould. Counterpart and companion at the same time, he is the ever-enthusiastic dreamer; idealistic, a little chaotic and seemingly rather aimless. He is full of astonished inquisitiveness, not phlegmatic – but still with a *laisser faire* mentality – and he is a proud father.

Distributed to the trade in North America by
North Light Books
an imprint of F&W Publications, Inc.
1507 Dana Avenue
Cincinnati, OH 45207
(800) 289-0963

Introductory photos:
p. 2/3: Let the finale begin: the last corner before the Salathé Headwall, IX/5.12d
p.4: Alexander on the huge dyno of his route Om in the Berchtesgaden Alps, XI/9a
p. 5: Thomas enjoying the exposure on the Salathé Headwall on El Capitan, X-/5.13b
p. 6/7: The Dolphin, an eyecatching feature on the upper third of El Niño on El Capitan
p. 8/9: Toni Gutsch and falling snow on the West Face of Latok II, Pakistan
p. 10/11: Kang Tega and Thamserku, two six thousanders above Namche Basar in the Khumbu Himal, Nepal

Photo credits:
Conrad Anker: p. 85 top
Dietmar Benz: p. 67 bottom right
Volker Benz: p. 67 bottom left
E. Birnbacher: p. 45
M. Brackenhofer: p. 70
Mark Chapman: p. 5, 22/23
Ruta Flohrschütz: p. 67 top
Toni Gutsch: p. 83
Hans Christian Hocke: p. 64/65, 66 right, 68/69
Alexander Huber: p. 8/9, 10/11, 24/25, 32, 54/55, 58, 61, 66 middle, 66 bottom., 71 right, 74 top, 78 right, 79, 82, 88/89, 90 (2), 91 (2), 92 (2), 93 (2), 94 (2), 95 (2), 96 bottom, 97, 107, 120, 121, 122, 123, 124, 125 (3), 126, 127, 128 top, 128 bottom
Thomas Huber: p. 14/15, 27, 28, 29, 39, 63, 70 top, 71 left, 72, 73, 74 bottom, 75 (2), 76, 77 (2), 78 left, 80, 81, 84 (2), 85 bottom, 86 (5), 101, 102, 128 middle
Thomas Huber senior: p. 34, 35 bottom (3)
Peter Mathis: p. 36/37, 38, 46, 50, 51, 52, 53
Matej Mejovsek: p. 103
Jan Mersch: p. 56/57, 59, 60, 62, 64, 118/119
Georg Simair: p. 96 top
R. Weithmann: p. 35 top
Heinz Zak: p. 2/3, 4, 6/7, 12/13, 14, 16, 17, 19 (2), 21, 40 (2), 41 (2), 42 (2), 44, 47, 48/49, 98/99, 104, 105, 106, 108, 109, 110, 111, 112, 114, 117

The authors and publisher would like to thank all the photographers for their cooperation and assistance.
The sketched topos on p. 21, 80 and 115 ff. are the work of the authors; the topo on p 104 is reproduced by kind permission of the magazine *klettern*.

Cover shots: Heinz Zak (front), Alexander Huber (back)

First published in German as: The Wall: Die neue Dimension des Kletterns by BLV Publishers Ltd Munich Vienna Zurich

First published in the UK 2001
Copyright © 2000 BLV Ltd, Munich
English translation © 2001 David & Charles

Translation: Tim Carruthers

A catalogue record for this book is available from the British Library

ISBN 0 7153 1178 6

Printed in Germany
For David & Charles, Brunel House, Newton Abbot, Devon

ROUTE GRADES

UK Trad	UK Tech	French	USA	Aus	UIAA
VS	4c	5a	5.8	18	6-
HVS		5a	5b	5.9	19	6
E1	5b	5c	5.10a	20	6+
		6a	5.10b		7-
E2		6a+	5.10c	21	7
	5c	6b	5.10d		
E3		6b+	5.11a	22	7+
		6c	5.11b		
E4	6a	6c+	5.11c	23	8-
		7a	5.11d	24	8
E5		7a+	5.12a	25	8+
	6b	7b	5.12b	26	
		7b+	5.12c	27	9-
E6		7c	5.12d		9
	6c	7c+	5.13a	28	9+
		8a	5.13b	29	
E7		8a+	5.13c	30	10-
		8b	5.13d	31	10
E8	7a	8b+	5.14a	32	10+
		8c	5.14b	33	11-
E9		8c+	5.14c	34	11
E10	7b	9a	5.14d	35	11+